Technology Entrepreneurs and Intrapreneurs' Handbook

A Roadmap with Directions from Creative Concept to Revenue and Profits

Don Perrine

The author gratefully acknowledges the permission given to reproduce copyright material. The author has made every effort to trace copyright material and obtain permission to use such material. If there have been any errors or omissions, the author apologizes and requests that such information be forwarded for inclusion in future printings.

For comments or questions, contact the author at: DonaldPerrine@gmail.com.

ISBN-13: 978-1517302443
ISBN-10: 1517302447

Printed by CreateSpace in the United States of America

Acknowledgements

I thank the reviewers who invested their valuable time and knowledge to help make a better product for the benefit of our readers.

Dr. Randolph Henke is the founder of Adarza Biosystems, Inc., Phyton Technologies, and Container Technologies Industries. Also, he was an Entrepreneur in Residence at High Tech Rochester.

Dr. John Langan is the founder of Computational Sensors Corporation and Superconducting Technologies, Inc.

John Morris is the founder of NetLearning, Inc. and Clearpath Ventures; also he was the CEO of Tech2020, a regional entrepreneurial accelerator.

M. Gary Verholek is the founder of Environmental Consulting Group and Industrial Process Services, Inc.

I also thank my wife, JoAnne Perrine, for her assistance in editing, her patience and her support in writing this book.

Table of Contents

Introduction

The purpose of this book is to enable entrepreneurs, intrapreneurs, product managers, senior managers and others engaged in the commercialization of technology products and services to think through critical aspects of the commercialization process. Yet, why should anyone care?

Technology entrepreneurs have a 1 in 10 chance of success, according to Rory Carroll's article on Silicon Valley published in The Guardian, and corporate intrapreneurs have an even lower success rate. So the reader's reason to care might be simply moving the odds of success in their favor! This book can serve as a:

- Roadmap of what to expect at each step to commercialization;

- Source of conceptual information about each step;

- Plan for high and mid-level actionable detail on each step;

- Resources recommendation for each step's more detailed understanding and implementation.

There are many books that speak to different pieces, each going into great depth and offering valuable insights. However, few if any offer the overview that puts it all together into a complete, common-sense picture. Often technology entrepreneurs and intrapreneurs have technical backgrounds, yet find themselves facing integral roles in the commercialization of a technology. For them, the material in this book should be especially useful. For example, it's worth noting that both my education and career's early stages were weighted heavily towards technology, but then shifted over time to supporting, then managing and leading various aspects of technology businesses. While my career was successful by many measures, I believe that much more could have been achieved had I been able to learn and fully understand earlier many of the points offered in this book.

"The most common thing about common sense is that it's not very common." – Author's version of quotes from Voltaire, Will Rogers, et al.

Another intention is that this book can be used as a handbook; that is, it can be either read or accessed for specific topics that may be relevant at any time. It should cause the reader to think about processes and topics they may have overlooked. All of the topics are treated at a fairly high level, deliberately. The reader hopefully will be stimulated to think through what must be done and seek out additional information until satisfied that a reasonable understanding exists and, therefore, the indicated steps to success can then be put in place and executed. Located at both the end of each chapter and in the References and Resources chapter at the end of the book there is a list of books, articles and web sites that can provide the finer detail and background for a deeper understanding. Also, in a few places material is repeated for the reader's convenience because it is relevant to more than one subject.

One takeaway that might come from using this book is the family of "mental models" that can serve as a framework for the more detailed work that one must do. They will provide at least an awareness of each ones' value and perhaps serve as a starting point. Another is discovering some ideas that are "gems". I've found often when taking courses or reading books on various subjects. Sometimes just a few valuable ideas make the whole experience worthwhile. An extreme example to illustrate the point, but to which I make no attempt to compare this work, is Warrant Buffett's annual reports – a veritable treasure trove of gems.

In this overall spirit, I've learned that we must see things differently at times, in order to overcome obstacles that are keeping us from realizing its full potential when commercializing a technology. While there are many "brain teasers' around, along with tricky IQ questions, I've chosen the one below to help the reader see how what appears to be challenging is actually very simple. Einstein said, and I must paraphrase, that anyone can make something complicated, but only a genius can make it simple. In my experience, we don't all need to be geniuses, but we do need to see things in unconventional ways that reflect the genius to simplify. So here it is:

$$62-63=1$$

Move only **one number** to make the equation correct.

The answer is not in the book, because frequently the answers to challenges must come from within. Perseverance is also a trait that I've found to be essential in overcoming obstacles and driving one to see things differently, and therefore, often simply. Once you realize how simple the answer really is, you may wonder why you didn't see it sooner. There is one hint that might be worth mentioning, while the answer is simple, the thought process leading to the answer is not everyday thinking.

In one of the companies I cofounded, our business was a conundrum: It was analogous to the early days of automobiles where the metaphorical question of the chicken or the egg was present for a long time. Saying it differently as an analogy: how can one sell cars when there are no gas stations? Or conversely, how can one sell gas when there are no cars? Indeed, a perfect conundrum. In our case, it was how is it possible to sell radiopharmaceuticals when there are no imaging devices to use them; and of course the converse was true. We did manage to resolve the market model dilemma eventually, but not without a lot of pain and time. We focused on areas that had the most likely probability of becoming major markets and invested a great deal in market development. Oh, and at the same time we had to work with the FDA to get approval for the manufacture of the radiopharmaceuticals for distribution as well as work on getting third party insurers to reimburse for various diagnostic imaging procedures. Fertile ground for innovative solutions and perseverance.

Stages of Technology and Manufacturing Risks

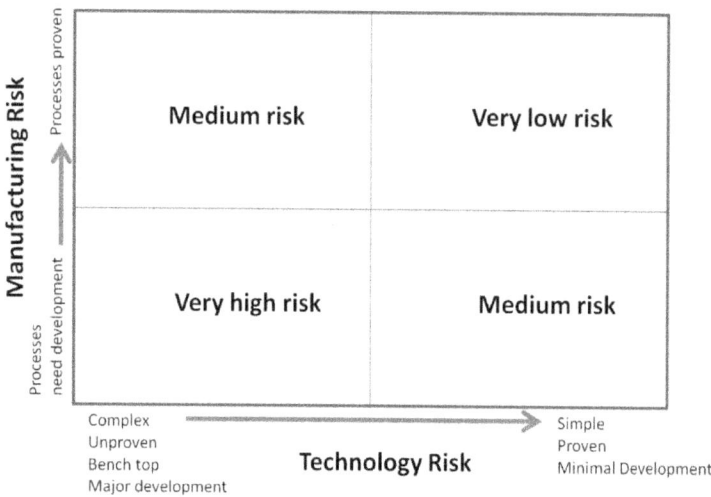

This leads to a point that should be considered when contemplating commercialization of a technology. The diagram above shows conceptually the relationship between manufacturing risk and technology risk.

Of course, technology and manufacturing risks should be considered within the context of market risks. This subject is addressed in the Market chapter. However, apart from the intricacies of markets, it is worth sharing a high-level quote from Dr. Lee Martin, a former colleague and technology entrepreneur, who said: *"You want to be just 20 minutes before your time"*. If the technology or manufacturing capability or market conditions will not fully support your product or service, you may be either too early or will have to do additional development work.

In one company that I help found, the technology was based on software platforms that existed. Therefore, the risk to manufacture was minimal while the technology risk resided in the ability to develop the specific content-related programs that would fulfill their value proposition. In addition, the specific operating programs and course content could be readily modified to either suit specific customer requirements or to introduce improvements – to amplify this point, note that reportedly since 2000, the cost of creating software companies has fallen by 10 times! By contrast, hardware is much more difficult and expensive to develop and/or modify. For reference, the value proposition was to provide computer-based learning in place of instructor-led, classroom training for regulatory-required practices in hospitals. In other words, they offered "better learning at lower cost". Not surprisingly, the company became successful in a relatively short time, and it was eventually acquired by a major player in the training and education market.

In contrast to that company, another of the companies that I co-founded had a long-wave infrared detector technology that was based on micro-electrical mechanical systems (MEMS). It required equipment and processes to micro-machine structures in silicon carbide that were layered over their corresponding semiconductor circuits. The technology risks were many, but to illustrate, one of the most important was that the physics are different for micron-size pixels in a detector array compared with the laws of physics for large objects. Our detectors had multiple pixel arrays in the 20-50 micron range that were required to behave in a predictable, reliable manner. In addition, the technology had only been demonstrated at the bench top level, so the amount of effort to bring the technology to where it was ready for manufacturing and commercialization was significant. Similarly, at the manufacturing level, the equipment and processes available at that time for MEMS had to be pushed to new limits in order to meet the requirements for commercialization. In summary, this company's technology and manufacturing risks were very high.

The intent of this topic is to sensitize the reader to the need to openly assess both of these risks thoroughly when planning to develop a technology for commercialization. Interestingly, the researchers who often perform the early stage breakthroughs at the bench-top or proof-of-principle level commonly see the amount of effort needed to develop the technology for commercialization as being minor; yet the truth is the opposite. Often it requires many multiples of effort and resources to carry it from proof-of-principle to being manufactured as a marketable product. Our teams in times past often cited the notion that no matter how well you plan, it takes twice as long, is twice as hard and takes twice as much resource – however, occasionally we were certain the coefficient was more than two!. These thoughts should not be discouraging in any way; rather they may help to better assess and manage the risks, resulting in a much higher probability of a successful outcome.

An empirical yet somewhat obvious notion might be considered here, wherein the position held by an idea in the above matrix has a relationship to its expected impact in its target market. In other words when considering pursuing an idea, the level of difficulty might seem daunting; but if its expected impact on the market is great, it may serve to justify the risk and effort. Milton Friedman reportedly said: *"The only theory in which economists are in universal agreement is that the value of an asset is determined by the expected benefits it will generate"*. This idea can be also valuable when looking for angel or venture funding.

Four interesting quotes offer some philosophical perspective on risk:

"The dilemma is that if one does not risk anything one risks even more." - Erica Jong

"Risk more than others think is safe. Care more than others think is wise. Dream more than others think is practical. Expect more than others think is possible." - Cadet Maxim, West Point, New York

"Something that is never put at risk loses its value." - Sigfrid Siwertz

"An idea that does not involve any risks is hardly worthy to be called an idea." - Oscar Wilde

Recently, the notion of Knowledge Based Capital has been discussed. The interesting point here is that technology commercialization is based on knowledge or intellectual property, which is not counted at this time in economic performance measures, such as gross domestic product (GDP). Therefore, both its importance and its contribution are not fully recognized among all who measure and all who are influenced by such measurements.

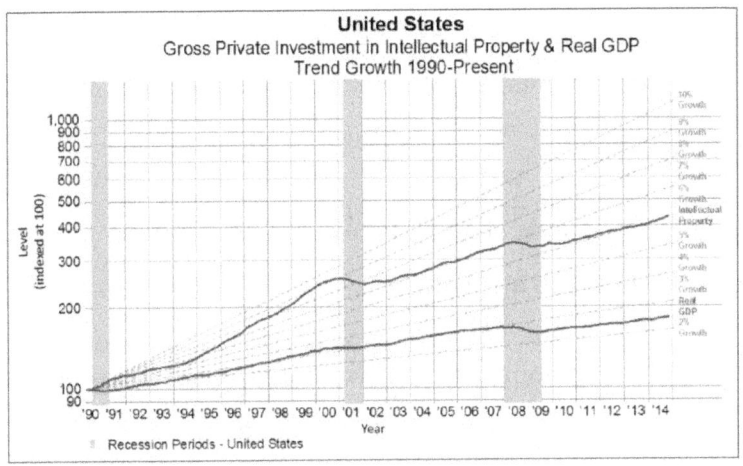

The chart above used with permission from Gavekal Capital, with a hat tip to Cam Hui, illustrates their view that the world is undergoing an innovation boom. Anyone working in the field of technology innovation may find this chart inspirational on a high level, because we must maintain our ability to innovate and create value. This notion applies both to our national economy and the world economy. While each country may see it as a "race to the top", it is one where all participating nations and economies can benefit the most; but even non-participating economies can benefit when they simply employ the products and services borne out of other's innovation.

Takeaways from the Introduction chapter:

- Having a roadmap to go from a vision to profitable commercialization can improve the likelihood of success

- Non-conventional thinking may help overcome obstacles along the way

- Technology and manufacturing risks need to be well understood, as well as market risks

- The potential "rewards" should outweigh the "probable risks" by some significant amount

- Knowledge based capital recognition needs to move beyond a company's balance sheet to show its contribution to GDP

Resource recommendations for more depth on this Introduction chapter:

- Adams, Rob. *If You Build It, Will They Come?* John Wiley & Sons, 2010.

- Carroll, Rory. *Silicon Valley*, theguardian, June 28, 2014.
  http://www.theguardian.com/technology/2014/jun/2

8/silicon-valley-startup-failure-culture-success-myth

- Smialek, Jeanna. Here's How Much Technology Is Messing Up Our Most Important Measurements of the Economy, *Bloomberg Business*, July 28, 2015. http://www.bloomberg.com/news/articles/2015-07-28/here-s-how-much-technology-is-messing-up-our-most-important-measurements-of-the-economy

Introduction

Plan for Success Process

"He that knows not, and knows not that he knows not is a fool.

Shun him

He that knows not, and knows that he knows not is a pupil.

Teach him.

He that knows, and knows not that he knows is asleep.

Wake him.

He that knows, and knows that he knows is a teacher.

Follow him."

Arabic proverb

I often observe folks driving who must merge onto an Interstate highway from an on ramp. The most common practice today is to just come up the ramp, not look to the traffic on the highway, but rather assume somehow you'll fit in. It's pretty risky and results in the traffic flow being distorted along with the occasional accident. This analogy compares with the notion of just implementing a new product or service without any more comprehensive planning. For example, a safe way to enter a fast moving highway is to visualize yourself finding a space in the oncoming traffic, then making it your mission to match the speed of traffic in such as way that you fit in followed by implementing the tactics. The result should be a smooth, safe merge.

The above Plan for Success chart is pretty comprehensive at the 30,000 foot level, which is exactly its purpose. The idea that the difference between one's vision and reality is a gap can be helpful in seeing more clearly two "dots" that must somehow become connected. Thus, the mission becomes the overall mechanism for connecting those two dots and getting to the vision. Similarly, key elements to completing the mission and realizing the vision are a good plan to close the gap, implementation discipline and adaptability/flexibility.

It's worth a comment on discipline and adaptability and flexibility. While a good plan supported by research, facts and understanding is critical, during the implementation phases the environment can change as well as new information discovered; in addition, sometimes the best of plans just don't work very well. Consequently, plan and implementation corrections need to be timely recognized and made.

Since I row a boat for pleasure and health reasons, I often see young men and woman rowing competitively. Competitive rowing strikes me as a sport that illustrates with great clarity the importance of the above concepts. When teams row, they use their ability to move in exact synchrony while applying appropriate force and technique to propel the boat towards the finish line in order to win the race. A breakdown might look like this:

<u>Vision shared</u>: win the race

<u>Mission</u>: get to the finish line first

<u>Strategy</u>: practice, strength building, maybe something more

<u>Tactics</u>: precise, efficient, effective movement aided by coaching

Another important observation in this rowing example is that trained teams seem to perform without any apparent distractions, such as politics, personality conflicts and side agendas. Imagine if one of the team members was trying to undermine another team member – yet this happens in business, and it is especially prevalent in large companies where momentum masks inefficient and ineffective performances. Nearly all startups that I've either been part of or have observed benefit from minimal distractions, because survival depends on success. However, that alone speaks more to efficiency than effectiveness. It's one of the purposes of this book to optimize both efficiency and effectiveness in realizing new technologies' full commercial potential.

Takeaways from the Plan for Success chapter:

- There are six key steps that start with knowing where you want to go and ending with measuring and adjusting along the way
- Team work is critical to successful implementation
- Competitive rowing can serve as a "mental model" of team performance, requiring all six key steps to be effectively employed

Resource recommendations for more depth on this Plan for Success chapter:

- Greenleaf, Robert K. *Servant Leadership,* Paulist Press, 2002
- Scholtes, Peter R., Brian L. Joiner and Barbara J. Streibel. *The Team Handbook, 3rd Edition*, Oriel, Inc., February 2003
- Vannelli, Steven and Eric Bush. *"The Knowledge Effect: Excess Returns Of Highly Innovative Companies",* Seeking Alpha, May 11, 2015 http://seekingalpha.com/article/3167886-the-knowledge-effect-excess-returns-of-highly-innovative-companies

Vision - Description of the Destination

My vision for this book came about from my experience both working with and being an entrepreneur and corporate intrapreneur in technology fields. I both experienced in myself and saw in others the weakness that came from not seeing the entire process at some level – either knowing that one doesn't know or not knowing that one doesn't know. Either way, the likelihood of success is reduced and the level of effort is increased. Thus, the vision for this book is to be: "A roadmap that will improve the odds of success for technology entrepreneurs and intrapreneurs".

The late Ned Herrmann, who was a physicist by training and a psychologist by persuasion, identified the below series of steps in the creative process. He taught this material in his creativity workshops, which were tied in with his work on the book *The Creative Brain*, published in 1989. One way or another we go through the above steps in getting to an idea or "vision". The preparation phase is one where information is gathered. It might be as simple as observing either an existing problem or user "angst" in some situation. Angst is sometimes identified as the reason an idea came to someone's mind. In a more complex situation, preparation might comprise doing some level of

21

engineering, scientific or other research that leads to an epiphany or "Aha" moment that solves some need or problem; or it can lead to a whole new idea that no one realized was even possible.

Vision and the Five-Step Creative Process

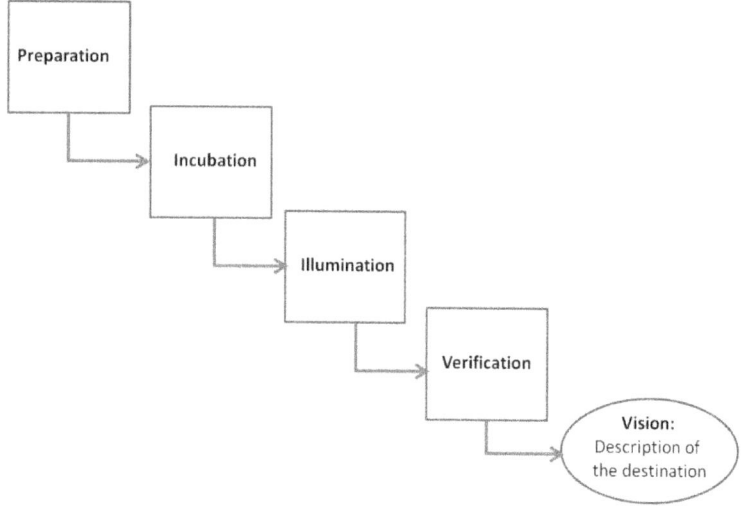

The next phase is the incubation phase. Einstein once said that he got his best ideas when he was eating an apple. I think what he meant was that having gone through continuous preparation associated with always working on some physics or math research, his knowledge would "percolate" in the back of his mind until the illumination phase produced an eureka or "Aha" moment. Saying it differently, it's a process whereby one's mind just needs to sort through all of the information until an epiphany pops out – it can't be forced. There is also a notion that if one can't get to an answer or eureka moment, perhaps there isn't enough information; so more preparation needs to be done.

The verification phase is when the solution is tested in some way to verify that it will provide an either an answer to a real problem that needs to be solved or create an entirely new opportunity. Verification might take the form of a bench-top experiment or could be done with market or some other research. In any case, the conclusion of the verification phase should be that the idea or vision is both worthy and doable.

Developing a Shared Vision

In a business setting where a team must work to achieve a vision, success from implementation becomes much more likely when all of the key employees or team members share in that vision. From my experience, a shared vision must be worthy of team members' effort to work hard in attaining its success, and it must be well understood to the point where there is deep assimilation or internalization. We've been successful doing this by team members

23

working on the planning and implementation as well as through workshops where the purpose is discussed, alternatives are considered and expected outcomes are evaluated. For example, in diagnostic imaging, a unique test that will improve the diagnostic accuracy compared to competing, established methods has a significant impact on health care and the affected population segment's quality of life. The idea that such outcomes are so important means that they are compelling and worthy by definition; and the idea that they will displace less effective current practices provides further motivation. In summary on this point, developing a shared vision among key, if not all, team members can make the difference between folks who show up to "do their job" and folks who are driven to succeed themselves through the success of the whole team.

An example that impressed me during the early recovery phase of the Great Recession of 2008 was from the CEO of Panera. He was asked why his company was growing revenue and profits when other companies were struggling to survive. His answer was simple: We provide great food that is good value, but also we ensure that our customers have a great experience. What struck me was how simple yet powerful was that vision statement. It seemed to me that every employee could understand it and frame their behavior based on it. I can also testify that every Panera experience we've had fits exactly the CEO's vision.

A friend recently told me about several non-profit, technology-facilitating organizations that he was working with to achieve a broad goal. He said that the organizations were caught up in competing agendas and turf issues. As a result, very little was being accomplished. I asked if these organizations had a shared vision of what they were trying to accomplish; the answer was no. I have worked with organizations that had competing visions among different functional parts of the organization. Even though the company's vision and mission were clear the level of infighting was extraordinarily self-destructive. The fact that the vision was not shared among the team was not recognized by the senior leadership, so it was "managed" rather than being corrected through leadership. When I would bring this to the attention of our board or the rest of our senior management, the answer, amazingly, was: *"it may seem crazy but it works"*. And it did work, until it didn't anymore; then a change would be made. In other words, typical of large institutions, change only comes when there is a crisis. I left the company years ago, and I suspect that the leaderships' attitude remains the same today.

One last thought on this point is that there is an old expression about teams when they come together to work on something. There are four phases:

- Forming
- Storming
- Norming
- Performing

I believe that the storming stage is driven by mixed views of what needs to be done as well as competing agendas. It is hard to imagine that every reader has not seen this often. When a shared vision is developed amongst the group, it moves from Storming to Norming; that is coming together around a central view of where the group needs to go. That enables the development of a plan so that the group can perform to close the gap between current reality and the shared vision.

What are the success elements of a vision statement?

- Clear and simple – I can understand it
- Worthy – I can support it
- Inspires and excites – I can do it and make a difference

Vision - Description of the Destination

Some various ways to define a vision:

- Articulate the purpose, direction and capabilities of the business; or do it for a specific product or service.
- Refer to a future state and condition that does not presently exist and never existed before.
- Relate it to customers.
- Distinguish it from competitors.
- Present its desired image.
- Express its commitments to stakeholders.
- Reflect in it the values and priorities of the leaders.
- Describe the difference we want to make in the world; i.e. the vital goal that animates us as we pursue our mission and adhere to our policies.

Some more examples of a vision:

- *There by 10:30 AM* – a former FedEx vision
- *News while it's happening* – a founding CNN vision
- *Buyer for the nation's homemaker* – I recall it was Sears earlier vision
- *"I have a dream...."* – Dr. Martin Luther King's famous quote

27

- *"People can find and discover anything they want to buy online"* – Amazon
- *"To give people the power to share and make the world more open and connected"* – Facebook
- *"Google provides access to the world's information in one click."* – Google

Another example is from Satya Nadella, Microsoft's CEO, who recently revised Microsoft's vision in the following:

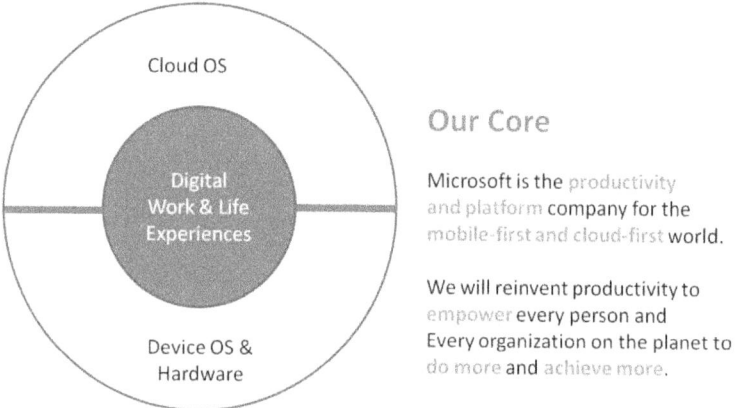

To illustrate the evolution of vision statements, consider this earlier one from Microsoft:

"A computer on every desk and in every home; all running Microsoft software."

An interesting historical contrast that may emphasize the importance of appropriate and meaningful vision statement is that around this same time, as I recall, Ken Olsen who was the founder and CEO of the now defunct Digital Equipment Corporation (DEC) reportedly said: *"I cannot see why anyone would want a personal computer in their home!"*

Here is a recent one from Tim Cook at Apple:

"We believe that we are on the face of the earth to make great products and that's not changing. We are constantly focusing on innovating. We believe in the simple not the complex. We believe that we need to own and control the primary technologies behind the products that we make, and participate only in markets where we can make a significant contribution. We believe in saying no to thousands of projects, so that we can really focus on the few that are truly important and meaningful to us. We believe in deep collaboration and cross-pollination of our groups, which allow us to innovate in a way that others cannot. And frankly, we don't settle for anything less than excellence in every group in the company, and we have the self-honesty to admit when we're wrong and the courage to change. And I think regardless of who is in what job those

values are so embedded in this company that Apple will do extremely well."- Tim Cook, CEO of Apple Computer as reported by Forbes.

While this vision statement is clear, it appears to combine vision, mission and various strategies all rolled into one.

Still, in these examples it isn't clear how much senior management, employees and other so-called stakeholders share any of these vision statements. Getting the vision clear and simple is of first order importance, but getting buy-in, either by up-front participation, education or another means puts power behind the words. In the example of Martin Luther King's vision, he built extraordinary power behind the words that both described and elaborated his vision. It helps make the case for the power of an idea, internalized by the very people who can make the vision reality!

"One idea lights a thousand candles". Ralph Waldo Emerson

A shared vision can take on more meaning when reinforced with a sharing of benefit, such as either stock options or restricted stock. While such sharing is no substitute for intrinsic motivation derived from buying into a shared vision, training, support and clear objective setting, they can be especially effective in early-stage companies where much is at personal risk; and often exceptional creativity, risk-taking, dedication and effort is required to accomplish the longer term vision and mission.

Organization Without a Shared Vision

Organization With a Shared Vision

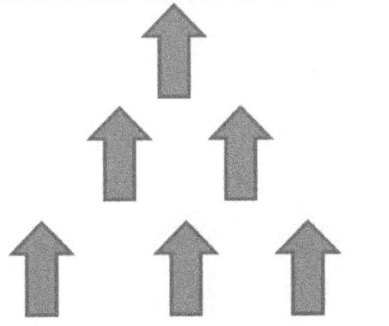

In summary, a shared vision is the organizational internalization of the vision; it satisfies the need for organizational clarity about its purpose and direction. Its value is that it feeds dynamic tension, guides the development of the mission; and it shapes the strategic and tactical plans. It clarifies the main signals from the daily noise in both planning and implementation, it can invoke deep belief, passion, and commitment; plus it inspires when others have doubt.

Takeaways from this Vision chapter:

- Creativity is a natural process that must be fed and nurtured
- A vision that is worthy will motivate, focus and inspire
- A shared vision puts the power to achieve behind the words

Resource recommendations for more depth on this Vision chapter:

- Gallo, Carmine. *The Four Elements of an Inspiring Vision.* Bloomberg Business. November 25 2008. http://www.bloomberg.com/bw/stories/2008-11-25/the-four-elements-of-an-inspiring-visionbusinessweek-business-news-stock-market-and-financial-advice

- Hermann, Ned. *The Creative Brain.* Brain Books, September 1, 1989

- Hull, Patrick. *"Be Visionary; Think Big"*, Forbes, December 19, 2012 http://www.forbes.com/sites/patrickhull/2012/12/19/be-visionary-think-big/

- Scholtes, Peter R., Brian L. Joiner and Barbara J. Streibel. *The Team Handbook, 3rd Edition*, Oriel, Inc., February 2003

- Vision Statement resource: http://www.lifehack.org/articles/work/20-sample-vision-statement-for-the-new-startup.html

Vision - Description of the Destination

Mission - Vision Minus Current Reality

"Would you tell me, please, which way I ought to go from here?"

"That depends a good deal on where you want to get to," *said the Cat.*

"I don't much care where—" said Alice.

"Then it doesn't matter which way you go," said the Cat.

"—so long as I get SOMEWHERE," Alice added as an explanation.

"Oh, you're sure to do that," said the Cat, "if you only walk long enough."

From Lewis Carroll's Alice in Wonderland

Here is a way to think about where you're going versus where you are. By assessing the current reality, it not only defines the gap, but it also creates dynamic tension. While dynamic tension is a phrase popularized by Charles Atlas in the 1920s to describe a group of exercises, it has been often co-opted for application to various business situations. The purpose here is to provide a label for the latent or potential energy created by the knowledge of where one needs to be in the future versus where they are at this time. In planning, this energy is released as kinetic energy helping drive the development of an effective plan; then drive the plan's implementation.

Mission: Vision minus current reality

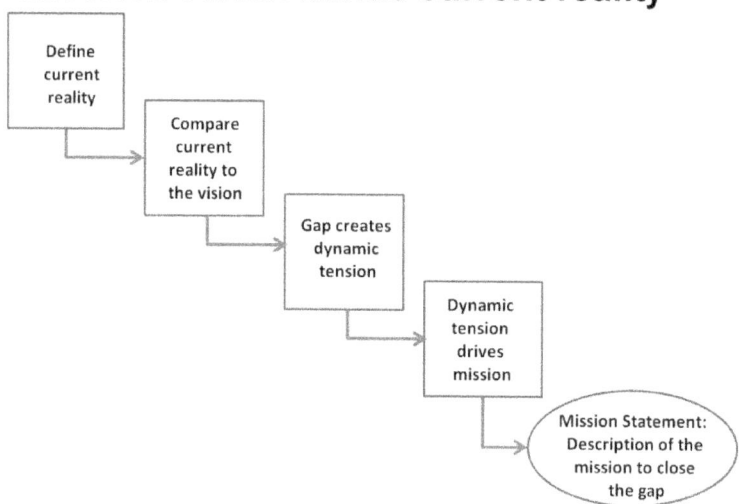

An example of key points in our mission at startup from the radiopharmaceutical company I cofounded, and mentioned earlier, was the following:

Vision: We will be the premier supplier of radiopharmaceuticals to customer-owned, regionally-located imaging centers throughout the United States and selected countries overseas. Our products, services and prices will be sufficiently attractive that no clinical diagnostic center located in our area of distribution would be incentivized to have their own radiopharmacy.

Current reality: No stand-alone clinical diagnostic imaging centers exist at this time. No FDA approval exists at this time for the manufacture and distribution of our short-lived radiopharmaceuticals. Medicare, Medicaid and third-party insurers do not routinely reimburse for most diagnostic imaging procedures using short-lived radiopharmaceuticals. The technology and processes exist for the production of all of our radiopharmaceuticals; however, commercial production processes and distribution systems must be developed.

Gap: Need to install regional radiopharmacies. Need to develop customers. Need to have customer's radiologist prescribe the required radiopharmaceutical under the FDA's Practice of medicine/Practice of pharmacy exemption while working with the FDA to obtain approval for the manufacture and use of these radiopharmaceuticals. Need to work with Medicare to obtain reimbursement approval for the diagnostic procedures that our customer will do; Medicare reimbursement will lead to other third party insurers following them. We must develop production processes and distribution processes.

Dynamic tension: Given the size and breadth of the gap, a lot was needed!

Mission: Build a strong organization to close the **Gap** by ensuring customers' success, thereby inspiring customers to become our shadow sales force. "Their success will be our success".

A longer term comment on Mission is that it can change over time due to many reasons, such as changes in the environment or the vision changes or the mission is "accomplished" to some significant extent so it needs to be revised. Interestingly, it's easy for a team to believe that a mission has been accomplished, such as George W. Bush's infamous aircraft carrier declaration of "Mission Accomplished" after invading Iraq. A business example is when a level of success in accomplishing a mission has been achieved, the team moves into an elegant facility, which then can send the message that they've "made it", and so now everyone can relax.

By contrast, in the early stages of technology startups, it seemed easy for everyone to share the vision and be committed to the mission. Team members by their own volition are more driven to do whatever it takes to succeed. There is little room for error and less room for petty politics and personal ambition that is so often found in larger, established companies. In other words, the chances of success are higher than may seem apparent at face value due to the likelihood that all team members are working together – there is a sense that "we'll all either succeed together or we'll fail together". I believe this is true even at the early stage when the vision is not yet clear; such as the case where an idea is very rough, but a lot of work must be done to have sufficient information to define a vision and mission.

Takeaways from this Mission chapter:

- Mission is the vision minus current reality

- The gap between vision and mission creates dynamic tension that energizes implementation

Resource recommendations for more detail this Mission chapter:

- Covey, Stephen R. Principle Centered Leadership, Chapter 30. Summit Books, 1991

- Branson, Richard. Richard Branson on Crafting Your Mission Statement. Entrepreneur. July 22, 2013. http://www.entrepreneur.com/article/227507

Mission - Vision Minus Current Reality

Strategic Plan - Do the Right Thing

If you ask 100 people *"what is strategy?"* you might get as many different answers. In addition, strategy and tactics are often used interchangeably. So, a simple way to think about strategy is that it is "doing the right thing"! Tactics, since they are implementation steps, are defined in this context as "doing the thing right".

To offer a simple illustration of the two, imagine that:

- You are on one side of a river that flows at 2 miles per hour
- You must get to an exact spot on the other side
- The exact spot you must reach can only be attained from the water
- There is no other way but to swim at your maximum speed of 1 mile per hour

If you start your swim from the point opposite your exact destination, you'll wind up downstream from your destination. But if you start your swim upstream from your destination by 2 times the river's width, you'll arrive by water at the exact spot required. So, your strategy is to walk upstream, then swim across at 1 mph while the river carries you down at a speed of 2 mph in order to arrive at the target.

Tactical implementation requires that you carefully estimate the river's width; measure that distance times 2 when walking upstream, then you must swim at exactly 1 mph. Either a tactical mistake on any of these points or a surprise event will cause you to miss your target. However, you have strategically put the river's flow to work for you.

Imagine trying to cross the river at 1 mph while it carries you away from your target at a speed of 2 mph? Hopeless! No matter how well you swim at that speed, you will never succeed. And that is the point – if you have the right strategy, the tactics can be reasonably implemented to succeed. However, if you have the wrong strategy, it doesn't matter how hard you try, how you change your tactics or how long you work at it; success will be either difficult or impossible.

In this example, what is one way you could you mitigate the tactical risks? If you walked upstream somewhat more than 2 times the river's width, you could swim below your maximum 1 mph speed allowing your reserve speed to be used if needed to either compensate for any measurement errors or deal with any "surprises" (which are almost always negative). Alternatively, you could swim at your maximum 1 mph speed to build a time reserve in case you encounter surprises that cause a delay; if no delay, slow down and "coast" to your target destination.

In summary on this example, you've chosen a strategy that frames success for the tactical implementation step – especially if you build into your strategy room for surprises. By contrast, planning for perfection will likely deliver some level of disappointment before success is achieved.

Strategy Development Process

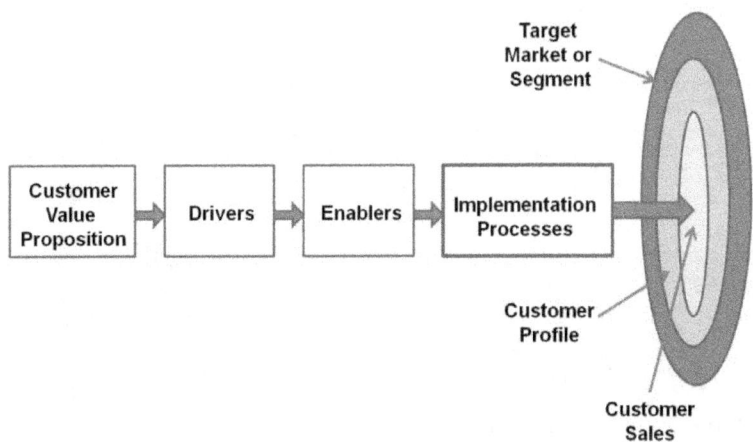

Similarly, in business, the strategy chosen will define and facilitate the pathway to follow for the implementation steps. However, to determine the best strategy requires information and knowledge. Any previous work on the vision, gap and mission will help, but other information about the technology and market are now needed.

Customer Value Proposition

Every marketer must wish that their competitors' value propositions were something like: *"You can buy a better product, but you can't pay a higher price"!*

Customer Value Proposition

One value proposition definition, courtesy of Investopedia, is: "A business or marketing statement that summarizes why a consumer should buy a product or use a service".

This statement should convince a potential consumer that one particular product or service will add more value or better solve a problem than other similar offerings." Forbes goes on to describe their five steps, which I've paraphrased for clarity, to establishing a value proposition as describing:

- Who are our target customers;
- That are dissatisfied with the current alternative(s);
- So will buy our new product or service;
- That provides the following key problem-solving capabilities;
- And that are unlike the current product or service alternatives.

The next step is to consider the adoption probability and rate. Often, this factor is couched in terms of a gain/pain ratio. Saying it differently, what will a buyer get in benefits versus all of the things that must be given up in addition to money? Some consider a value proposition's gain to pain ratio of 10 times to be the minimum for satisfactory adoption. I've always viewed a value propositions' gain versus pain issue in terms of customer value attributes and customer sacrifice attributes, as illustrated in the chart above.

Another way to say it is that the value proposition needs to maximize the value attributes (gain) and minimize the sacrifice attributes (pain). An example of this is the operating systems offered by Microsoft. My observation and experience with these products is that, among other issues, they create new versions that force a significant new learning curve on the buyer instead of building on existing customers' position on the Microsoft experience curve!

A significant sacrifice is that prospective buyers of a Microsoft operating system upgrade know that they will have to relearn the features and how can they be accessed and then used each time. In addition, Microsoft seems to be obsessed with the idea that their customers want them to anticipate and automate everything. While this thinking is likely grounded in an effort to strengthen their operating systems value attributes, for me and probably many others, it is a significant sacrifice because I have to find a "work-around" to get many things done the way I want to do them.

Microsoft's operating system product offering has certain value attributes, but to a large extent, they are offset by the sacrifice attributes. If they were starting out today with Windows, would they likely succeed? Note that in 1980,

IBM decided to not supply the operating system for their PC, subsequently selecting Microsoft to be the supplier according to Wikipedia's IBM DOS article. One could say that Microsoft got the "lucky card" or in other words, Microsoft received the "keys to the Magic Kingdom". Today, they benefit from the limited number of competing alternatives available to OEM, business and retail customers that are invested in the Microsoft-based platforms, cross-platform compatibility, upgradable products and the company's momentum.

In the case of software applications, friction is a concept that applies to either barriers or other sacrifice attributes associated with the use of the application. Interestingly, friction can be used as either an advantage or a disadvantage. For example, in an application for selecting a service such as Angie's List, a barrier to use is the fee that they charge. In some application products, friction is created by the consequence of employing a minimalist design, rendering the software product or app with a complex protocol for its use. An example that we are all familiar with on a different level is a microwave whose control panel is too minimalist making it non-intuitive; i.e. one needs to get out the manual each time it needs to be used for something different.

By contrast, friction can be used to advantage where a market for a complex or feature-rich product has become mature. It creates an opportunity for a lower cost, more minimalist product that can take market share away from the original feature-rich product. In other words, a competitor can enter the market both under the price umbrella created by the original offering and also under the "complexity" umbrella! However, while it would have higher friction or sacrifice attributes, one would expect that they would be a fractional trade off for the new benefit attributes that one would receive.

Customer Value Attributes

Harvard Business Review in a related article offers the following definition of customer value: "Value in business markets is the worth in monetary terms of the technical, economic, service, and social benefits a customer company receives in exchange for the price it pays for a market offering."

Note that I make a significant distinction between customer value, as defined above, and customer values, as defined and discussed below. The first is what is delivered;

the second is what deeply matters to target customers, thereby shaping their attitude and behavior.

Product or service offering ("it") and features and benefits: In describing what "it" is, consider that the features are meaningless unless they provide tangible benefit to your target customers. A way to semi-quantify those benefits is to talk about your product's or service's features with a sample of your target customers; ask them what benefit those features will provide. Then ask them to quantitate the benefits in some way; perhaps as time saved or better outcomes or ease of use, as examples. Also, consider forming an advisory board using representatives from your target customer base.

An excellent article adding information on this approach by Steve Blank is in the resource recommendations below. It covers the concept of a "Lean Startup". Essentially, the article describes an iterative process of starting with a concept or prototype, learning from target customers, and then evolving the product or service into one that will be adopted. This concept of Lean Startup contrasts with the more conventional "linear" approach, whereby a product is developed, then introduced to the market with the risk that it may not be the right fit.

<u>Customer needs and expectations:</u> Often these are pretty well known, if you have experience in the field where a new product or service is being offered. However, there can be surprises, and the thing about surprises is that they are usually not good. Surveys can be helpful when well designed and executed, but a simple telephone survey can also be valuable for gaining deeper insight. A technique I've used successfully is to identify about 15 or 20 target customers, make a list of about five key questions that will help you better understand their needs, expectations and problems. Then call each one, introduce yourself and the fact that you're doing a survey related to a planned product or service offering. Ask them if they can spare 15 minutes to respond to five questions. Almost always, folks will say yes. It is worth noting that Rob Adams in his book "If you build it, will they come?" suggests that the number of target customers to survey is 100. If this is a market that is new to you or the product or service is very complex or the investment is extremely high, then consider that more might be better. In Rob Adams' book, he also suggests repeating the interview process as the concept evolves and becomes refined; it's an idea that could be valuable with either the same group of interviewees or different ones each time.

As you move through the questions, the respondent may introduce new ideas, comments or other information that is valuable, but not related to the specific questions. I've found that by just following this new thread, major insights and ideas were gained. After 15 minutes, if more time is needed, I always ask if they can continue another five or ten minutes; it shows deep respect and appreciation for their time. After speaking with about 10 or so respondents, a pattern begins to emerge; additional calls tend to support the emerging pattern. The information gained will help shape your thinking about their needs, expectations and problems as well as introduce some new ideas. The information gained may lead to either more work to better understand this area or it may be sufficient to enable moving forward with the next steps in your plan.

Customer Values: If a reader only gets this concept from this book, I am convinced that his or her time spent reading it will pay huge returns! **What a customer needs, wants or expects is very basic;** by contrast however, **understanding customer values is strategic and can be game changing**. It goes beyond Joseph Schumpeter's concept of creative destruction, which MIT defines as "...the incessant product and process innovation mechanism by which new production units replace *outdated ones. It was coined by Joseph Schumpeter (1942), who considered it 'the essential fact about capitalism'."*

Oliver Wendell Holmes said: *"The mind once expanded to the dimensions of larger ideas never returns to its original size"*. This quote sums up the meaning of customer values. They are deep levels of importance that can be addressed with products or services that customers never knew they could have!

For clarification, we are using value in three different contexts – so here are definitions for each:

- **Customer Value** – benefit attributes minus sacrifice attributes. Ideally a large, positive quantity.
- **Value proposition** – Summary statement of a product or service's benefits minus sacrifices.
- **Customer values** – Customers' most basic beliefs that shape their attitude and behavior.

I learned from Steven Covey's book, the *Seven Habits of Highly Effective People*, that values drive attitudes and attitudes drive behavior. In other words, if one wants to change behavior, then work on attitude; if one wants to change attitude, then work on values!

Years ago, when we were all fixated on better amplifiers and better speakers and noise reduction technology and audiophile records for getting the best sound available, digital music suddenly became available on CDs. Within a very short time, vinyl records and all of their related technologies became obsolete; everyone bought CDs. Digital music changed the market overnight – because customers valued quality sound without noise (high gain/low pain)!

Another example, although not directly technology related but facilitated by it, is CNN. When Ted Turner founded the company, his vision was "news while it's happening". The old paradigm was that the news would be broadcast when it was received by tape or in some other form. Live news from anywhere in the world was enabled by satellites and bandwidth, and it changed viewers' expectations from the time it was made available. What did customers value? My guesses are:

- Knowledge – self actualization
- Security – feeling safer due to knowledge of potentially risky events; i.e. reduced uncertainty
- Social – able to discuss and opine

Another example is with Apple. In my view, Steve Jobs had an extraordinary innate ability to sense what his target customers valued, not just the more tactical "needs, wants and expectations". Every time Apple came out with a new product, the competition must have said: *"What just happened? Stop the R&D programs; our new designs in development are already obsolete."* Then they scrambled to "catch up", but usually never got out in front. Changing customer expectations through understanding customer values changes the game for all parties. I recall that Steve Jobs once said that he wanted to give customers products that they never knew they could have. The following quote from Steve Jobs and then one from Henry Ford highlight this idea.

"Market research can tell you what your customers think of something you show them. Or it can tell you what your customers want as an incremental improvement on what you have, but very rarely can your customers predict something that they don't even quite know they want yet." ~ Steve Jobs

"If I had asked people what they wanted, they would have said faster horses." ~Reportedly said by Henry Ford.

One last example worth mentioning is Netflix. They started around the year 2000 competing with DVD rental companies such as Blockbuster by offering a mail order service for DVDs that had better service and selection at a lower cost, and without the sacrifice attributes of Blockbuster. With Blockbuster, one had to drive to the store, spend time searching, return it to the store, and pay late fees. Then they took advantage of emerging broadband to offer streaming programming, which further strengthened their value proposition. Then at that time, they had attractive prices, strong benefit attributes through selection, convenience and instant delivery accompanied by almost zero sacrifice attributes other than cost. Now they're producing their own content. Their stock traded as low as 0.50 cents after going public in 2002, and as of this writing in 2015, it's trading around $130 with a market cap of $52 billion! What's next – will it be by them or to them?

One simple way to get a rough understanding of what your target customers value is to ask them what is important, and then ask them why. I've found that an informal technique of asking as many as six times *"Why is that important to you?"* after each explanation, like pealing an onion, helps reveal the most basic reasons.

Another approach is to predict what customer's value, then set about either confirming, modifying or rejecting the predictions based on personal interviews.

No matter how it's done, understanding customer values will be a tremendous asset in nourishing the creative process for new products and services, as well as repositioning existing ones.

Customer Sacrifice Attributes

Mainly folks think of price as the cost of receiving benefits. However, to quote Warren Buffett, *"Price is what you pay; value is what you get"*. In the construct of value there are a number of actual sacrifices that one has to make. Yet, this subject can be controlled to a large extent by awareness and design or development effort to minimize the sacrifices. Recalling from the chapter above, that some experts suggest a successful ratio is 10 times the gain versus pain or value versus sacrifice attributes. That is part of the challenge for anyone leading a new technology product or service.

<u>Time and Access to Understand</u>. While one example cited above is the Microsoft operating systems, another is an

investment advisory service to which I recently subscribed. Their web site showed compelling information about why their service would provide exceptional value, but when attempting to subscribe the first problem encountered was that, because I had once tried a "free trial" with them, my information was still on their server, so it would not allow me to use my own information to register. After contacting the company, their suggestion didn't work, but I did manage a work-around. Then, when looking for the exact product I wanted, it wasn't on the list of available subscriptions. Contacting them again, they sent me a PDF showing an updated list that hadn't made it to their website, along with how to subscribe. I wasted several hours, and had my confidence in them eroded by the experience. How often have you tried to use a website, but they make it so difficult, one way or another, that you either feel like giving up or actually do! Of course, we can each think of many examples across a broad spectrum of products and services where we've encountered similar issues.

Difficult to Use, Support, Service or Unreliable. An example of difficult to use is my son's experience with the latest Sony Play Station. He purchased it and enjoyed the excellent display and associated games. However, the controller ergonomics were so poor for him, that he developed pain in his hands that took weeks to heal. Consequently, he finally sold the device because the sacrifice of physical pain was more than the benefit received from an otherwise excellent product. One has to wonder, did they ever test the controllers with potential customers or focus groups? Package design experts with whom I've worked in the past believed that the most important area for care in design and deserving of significant investment are the human interface points of the package or product.

An example of difficult to support, is customer service. Many folks have had unsatisfactory experiences when calling a company's customer support and getting someone overseas who is looking at a computer screen with various questions and answers. But a more specific example for me is when we had cable service some years ago. Each time we tried to get help from their customer support, it was a complete waste of time. The last call we made was handled by a young person who clearly had no idea about the subject. We cancelled our service and subscribed to a satellite company.

Another example is when we built a semi-custom, ocean-going boat, I created a spare parts list and then placed an order with the boat builder's parts department. Two months later when I called about the status of some critical spare parts, the parts department manager said he didn't have them, but his defense was that he'd sent someone a memo two months earlier. It turned out that the Vice President of the company hired is son in law to be the new parts manager, a job for which he evidently had no previous qualifications. I finally got the parts by persevering, because when you're at sea, you don't pick up the phone and call for service – you must be largely self-sufficient. The interpretation I made from this experience was that the company thought more of this relative than it did of their customers' needs.

Regarding service and reliability, I have a strong belief that the root cause of many issues in this area is that the folks involved in the design, manufacture and writing of the manuals never use the products themselves. If they did, the products would be designed, built and documented very differently. Perhaps a "law" needs to be created that anyone working in these three areas should be required to use, service and maintain the products at least 30 days per year. Alternatively, this is an area that anyone leading a technology product or service can impact for their own company, and I predict that they will reap huge rewards.

I have often "dragged kicking and screaming" our engineers into the field in times past to speak with customers to observe what they do to gain a better understanding of their problems. The result has always been a better product or problem solution, because they are bright, capable people who need information and knowledge to do their jobs well.

One example of serviceability is on the diesel generator of our boat. It doesn't have an oil filter, but rather an oil screen. The manufacturer recommends cleaning the screen after every 500 hours of operation. The way that the screen is accessed is by – you guessed it – uninstalling the generator to access the underside of the unit. Could this level of sacrifice have been eliminated?

I am sure that the reader could spend hours if not days listing all of their experiences with service, maintenance and reliability issues. It is an area where significant reduction in sacrifice or pain can be made by a technology product or service leader. Interestingly, this area has a significant effect on customer attitudes and future behavior; and so, obviously, they will impact repeat purchase, brand equity and the long term adoption and acceptance of a product.

Fear, Uncertainty and Doubt (FUD)

How could "FUD" creep into a customer value proposition's sacrifice attributes? Two examples are either incomplete information or a lack of clarity in the description of the product or service.

I cannot begin to count the number of times I have decided to not purchase something because the information was not complete. Whether on the web or in a store, the lack of a complete description or specifications that would answer some examples of common questions:

- Will it fit the space available?

- Will it work with my current equipment?

- Do I need special cables or some other connection means?

The list of questions could be nearly endless. However, one effective way to ensure that FUD is minimized if not eliminated is to have the engineers, tech writers, service, marketing and manufacturing folks either "buy" and use the product or service. An alternative way is to observe some folks whose profile fits the least capable, early/late majority customer, and who has no involvement with the company, try to "buy" and use it for the first time. If it is all good for this type of customer, it should be a breeze for the rest of them.

A third way is using a beta test process. This will be discussed later as a powerful part of the customer's product or service adoption process. Essentially, part of what will be learned from having a group of early stage, partnered customers is the extremely valuable feedback and interaction.

Purchase and usage costs

It is worth repeating Warren Buffett's famous quote: "Price is what you pay, value is what you get." If price is viewed here as only the money exchanged; and value is narrowly defined here as the economic benefit, then the math becomes simple.

Consider the air transportation industry. Carriers are buying new planes on a regular basis, mainly because the newer designs are more fuel efficient, lighter and can carry more passengers per unit of operating cost. Merchant marine vessels are replaced for similar reasons. The short-term, tactical driver in this example might be getting to lower costs with higher profits. However, the strategic, long-term diver is survival because if you don't continually improve productivity, or in this case cost per mile or per passenger or per ton, your completion will do it, leaving you in a less competitive position.

Thus, the net economic benefit is a powerful component of a value proposition. Recall also from an earlier chapter that a 10X ratio of gain versus pain, or customer value attributes versus customer sacrifice attributes, is a good rule of thumb for successful adoption and market penetration.

Compelling reason to buy

The most dramatic scenario is one where a product or service will change customer expectations, because customer values were understood and creatively addressed. This compares with the more common approach of surveying customer needs and wants in order to offer a better product or service. The latter is always good; but the former is better.

Smartphones present an evolving series of compelling reasons to buy – a slow motion evolution. Historically, the first device that combined telephony, computing and a display was developed by Theodore Paraskevakos in 1971 and patented in 1974, according to Wikipedia's smartphone article. Yet, it wasn't until 1994 that IBM commercialized the first mobile phone and personal digital assistant (PDA). Starting in the late 1990s through the early 2000s, numerous companies offered different versions of smartphones including Nokia, Ericson, RIM's Blackberry, HP and Palm.

Mass adoption began with the introduction of NTT DoCoMo's smartphone in Japan, achieving 40 million users by 2001 within a total population of fewer than 150 million at that time! Although it took a long time for technology to catch up with the original idea, Japan's rate of mass adoption sends the obvious message that there was something very compelling about the product.

In 2007 Apple introduced the first iPhone with one of its differentiating advantages being the capacitive touch screen instead of the tiny keyboards that were a source of sacrifice for many users; the tiny keyboards were totally phased out by 2010. Then in 2008, HTC introduced the first phone based on Android's operating system. From 2008 through 2015, significant developments have been introduced by all smartphone suppliers that provide compelling applications on the smartphone platform – and it is indeed a platform technology in a broad sense.

Compelling application examples evolved to offer benefits in (not necessarily in temporal sequence):

- Connectivity – voice, text, email and web access anytime, anywhere
- Music – listen and manage your collections and selections
- Games – off-line individual and on-line individual and group
- Social – richer connectivity and social interaction
- Access – reservations, taxis, Uber, product ordering
- Photography and video – images and live streaming
- Finance – payments, account management, money transfers
- Business tools – reports, data, access, productivity
- Location – GPS tracking, directions, closest services
- GMS and CDMA standards – world access anywhere
- WiFi and Bluetooth – Off plan access with potentially higher bandwidth and wireless access to other devices

- Third party access – unlimited new apps
- Accelerometer – measure movement for health monitoring
- Storage – messages, photos, video, reports, data on the device or in the cloud

The platform technology that frames smartphones appears to follow Moore's Law, which was a prediction made in 1965 that the density of transistors per square inch on an integrated circuit would double each year for the foreseeable future – that was made 50 years ago! So while the smartphone is evolving as better, faster, and cheaper; and each new generation offers its own incremental improvements to mostly provide differentiating advantages, the most compelling reasons to buy are in the applications.

Apple appears to be the hands-down leader in the applications that are built on their platform that offers its own differentiating advantages. To support this point, consider that while Apple sold 20% of the world's smartphones in 2015, they dominate in operating profit of smartphones sales, taking a reported 92% of the top 8 world suppliers' smartphone profits in Q1 2015 versus 65% for the same period in 2014. For comparison, the next closest supplier was Samsung that took 15% of operating profits, which means that some suppliers are losing money, according to Seeking Alpha's citation of the wealth management firm Canaccord Genuity. Note that Apple's performance in the PC field is similar with 6% of the world's PC sales, they've garnered over 50% of the total fields' profits, according to Seeking Alpha's citation of Bernstein Research. Apple's performance speaks strongly to the importance and benefit of leading with at least some compelling applications and differentiating advantages that change customer expectations. Their performance also suggests that they succeeded in minimizing customer sacrifices while maximizing customer benefits. A possible bonus for Apple is that numerous reports imply that, among certain demographic groups, Apple products are a status symbol.

A possible framework for considering how compelling is a given value proposition would be Maslow's hierarchy of needs, summarized in the chart below.

In his later years, Maslow is reported to have added Self-transcendence to his hierarchy, which could be added to the top of the chart. He thought it captured the notion that the self only finds its actualization in giving itself to some higher goal outside oneself, in altruism and spirituality.

Maslow's Hierarchy of Needs

Chart used with permission and courtesy of Steve Roesler
Group www.steveroesler.com.

Critics claim that the hierarchical levels are not mutually exclusive, nor does one necessarily advance from the lowest to the highest without jumping ahead. For our purpose of using his hierarchy as a guide for clarifying or testing how compelling is a value proposition, it can be useful at face value.

Some examples follow:

- In countries where water is scarce due to contamination or overconsumption, a compelling reason to consider water desalinization or purification equipment addresses physiological needs. Can one survive without either clean or even just any water?

- In areas where crime is high, security systems are compelling because they address safety needs. Does anyone want to be a victim of a crime?

- In any society, the platform for social networking addresses the need for affiliation, belongingness and social interaction; ironically however, this appears to be true whether the outcome of such interactions is good or bad for society. Don't most folks, especially young people, want to be socially popular and connected?

- Any tools or education programs that enable improvement in one's profession, hobbies and other interests can be compelling because they address the need for self-esteem as well as self-actualization. Is an effective training course, relevant to one's profession, likely to be compelling? If it offers certification or a degree, is it even more compelling?

- A product like Rosetta Stone may offer a compelling way to enhance one's level of self-actualization through learning and mastering a foreign language. Saying it differently, Rosetta Stone can be a vehicle for satisfying one element of the dynamic tension caused by the current reality of one's vision to realize their full potential. Today's digital technologies provide the enabling platform for this product, which can be used by anyone, anytime, anywhere.

- If self-transcendence is a level above self-actualization, then is it possible that crowd funding or crowd sourcing is compelling, and popular, for those contributing, because it addresses the need for self-transcendence?

In summary, there are many ways one can refine and test a premise of a compelling reason to buy. For example, a few simple test questions are:

- What problem does it solve versus current competing solutions?

- Can its solutions' economic advantage be quantified?

- Can its other advantages be quantified?

- Does it either change prospective customers' expectations or is it an incremental improvement?

- It is worth investing effort on this subject, because it is very powerful and can overcome other weaknesses in a product or service's value proposition. Of course, it must be viewed in the context of competing alternatives.

Competing alternatives and differentiating advantages

In low-differentiated commodities markets the main advantage for volume sales is price. Generally, the lowest price supplier can get the most business; but the lowest cost supplier who competes on price will make a profit and get the most desirable business.

By contrast, products and services that are highly differentiated and sufficiently compelling command premium prices. Moreover, to the extent that they require minimal non-monetary sacrifices, then profits, adoption rates and market penetration become even more favorable. Of course, to the extent that the relative differentiating advantages are protected by intellectual property, in the form of either patents or trade secrets to create barriers to competitive entry, the product life cycle can be sustained longer by making low-risk investments in incremental improvements over time.

In one of the companies that I cofounded, we had patented technology for an infrared detector (IR) that would offer as a simple value proposition *"twice the performance at half the cost"*. It addressed the barrier to broad adoption for uncooled IR detector arrays, which was cost/price and limited performance for the most compelling applications where resolution and sensitivity were needed. Higher resolution meant more detail in the image for all applications (military, fire fighting, security, navigation, among many others), but without a new technology it meant proportionately higher cost. Higher performance at higher cost was a current competing value proposition, and therefore part of the market's problem. The same was true for higher sensitivity, who's main benefit was more "photons' or data in the image in a given amount of time. This was important for seeing through smoke and fog, for example, as well as improved image quality in all applications. Thus the value proposition of *"twice the performance at half the cost"* was both compelling and highly differentiating, while protected by patents and trade secrets.

Another example is the Dyson hand dryer seen in public restrooms. This device has differentiating advantages compared with paper towels, old style blowers and newer high-speed blowers. The Dyson device simultaneously dries both hands faster, with a single up and down pass, through the "blade" of air; and it is much quieter than either the older or the newer high-speed blowers. As a user, I'll choose it for those reasons over the other alternatives when available at a facility – i.e. faster drying with less noise.

For the owner or manager of restrooms - e.g. theaters, restaurants, parks, etc. – the Dyson's lower noise, more efficient process and happier users has obvious advantages, but the key might be the economic benefits; one being the need for fewer hand dryers, because each user is done in a few seconds versus the much longer time for both slow and fast blowers. Relative to paper towels, however, the economic differentiating advantages become extremely compelling. Paper towels are slow; users are in the restroom longer so more may be needed. They also require frequent attention, compared with Dyson's near zero maintenance. For example, paper towel dispensers incur the continuous cost of consumable paper used to constantly refill the dispenser; there mechanical parts need to be maintained; they require that receptacles for the waste paper be provided; then the waste paper receptacles must be emptied, along with cleaning up the waste paper that is dropped on the floor! It's interesting that such a mundane problem of drying hands in a restroom that could easily have gone unrecognized was advanced to a whole new level of efficiency and benefit for all parties by one technology company – Dyson.

The chart below, Product Strategy Matrix, summarizes some key points to consider based on the strength of a product or services' differentiating advantages versus a target customer's compelling reason to buy. In the ideal case where the relationship is High/High, there is an opportunity to create a success model. The success model's main benefit would be to enable future scalability and repeatability. For example, in the case where annexation can be done, whether geographic, moving up the value chain or by leveraging a platform technology to enter an adjacent field-of-use; the organizational structure, culture and supporting processes already will be in place.

By contrast, in the Low/Low case, harvesting or milking a cash cow might work for some time, thereby providing cash to either develop a stronger product or find other options for the business.

The High/Low case is one where often it's a solution looking for a problem. This is not unusual in my experience with technology products and services – sometimes R&D will come up with a technology that is clever, but the application connection hasn't been made yet, such as was the case with 3M's "Post-it" notes. Their low-tack, reusable, pressure-sensitive adhesive was developed by accident in 1968, but it took five years to find a compelling application for it. The challenge then in the High/Low case is to make it compelling for the target customers. That starts ideally with understanding what they value, then finding a way to provide those customers with something they never knew they could have. At a minimum, of course, just give them something that solves a very real problem better than any other product or service on the market.

Finally, in the Low/High case, this is a "me too" product or service, akin to a commodity. If you have lower cost than any competitor, you could do well; alternatively, one option is to find a way to develop a meaningful differentiating advantage versus the competition.

Product Strategy Matrix

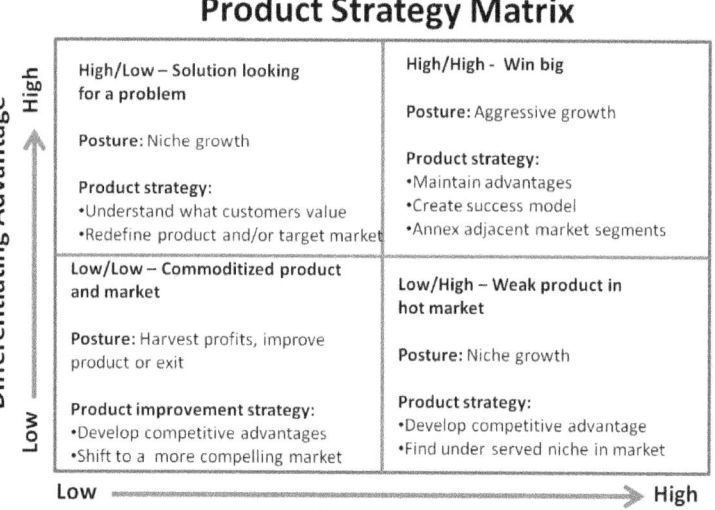

Takeaways from this chapter on Strategic Plan:

- Strategy is *"doing the right thing"* versus tactics which are *"doing the thing right"*

- Value proposition is a summary statement of a product or service's benefits minus sacrifices, which equals Customer Value

- Customer Values, by contrast, are the target customers' most basic beliefs that shape their attitude and behavior; understanding them can lead to game changing innovation

- Products and services must have a compelling reason for its target customers to buy and strong differentiating advantages relative to competing alternatives

Resource recommendations for more detail on this Strategic Plan chapter:

- Blank, Steve. Why the Lean Start-Up Changes Everything. *Harvard Business Review*, May 2013.
- https://hbr.org/2013/05/why-the-lean-start-up-changes-everything/ar/1
- Deneffe, D et al. *Overcoming the Real barriers to Entry into Adjacent Markets*, A.D. Little, January 2010
- Dunkley, Mike. *"Why we need to move up the value pyramid for health tech"*, VentureBeat.com. October 16, 2014. http://venturebeat.com/2014/10/16/why-we-need-to-move-up-the-value-pyramid-for-health-tech
- Grayeff, Yigal, Apple Inc. *(AAPL)*, *Seeking Alpha*, http://seekingalpha.com/news/2623855-apples-dominance-of-profit-almost-complete

- Stahl, M.J and Gregory M. Bounds, *Competing Globally Through Customer Value*, Quorum Books, 1991

- Vannelli, Steven and Eric Bush. *"The Knowledge Effect: Excess Returns Of Highly Innovative Companies"*, Seeking Alpha, May 11, 2015 http://seekingalpha.com/article/3167886-the-knowledge-effect-excess-returns-of-highly-innovative-companies

- Woodruff, Robert B. and Sarah Gardial. *Know your customer- New Approaches to Understanding Customer Value and Satisfaction*. Blackwell Publishers. 1996.

Marketing

As was the case earlier with strategy and tactics, I've observed that the terms marketing and sales are often used interchangeably. My own simple definitions are:

- Marketing: Creating demand
- Sales: Fulfilling demand

While this may seem an oversimplification, and it is to a certain extent, it is a very convenient way to see what must be done, how it must be done and who must do it. One illustration is that in a past corporate experience, our sales organizations worldwide were totally separated from the products-producing "factories" that also had marketing responsibility. It was often difficult to be effective in these conceptually complementary if not symbiotic roles. The reasons were that each party was not able to consistently respect the boundaries of the other party; however, had they been able to better understand and reasonably respect those boundaries, then that should have enabled them to be much more effective together.

To put a little more color on the subject, Business Dictionary.com offers the following definition for marketing:

"The management process through which goods and services move from concept to the customer. It includes the coordination of four elements called the 4 P's of marketing:

- *Identification, selection and development of a **product**,*
- *Determination of its **price**,*
- *Selection of a distribution channel to reach the customer's **place**, and*
- *Development and implementation of a **promotional strategy**."*

To compare the term <u>sales</u>, the same source provides the following definition:

- *"The activity or business of selling products or services*

  .

- *An alternative term for sales revenue or sales volume."*

While these Business Dictionary definitions are lacking a number of key responsibilities, one takeaway is that marketing is both strategically and tactically enabling (supportive); while sales is applying strategies and tactics that will effectively match prospective customers' needs with product or service solutions and closing the deal.

More specifically, I see the primary actions of the marketing function as follows.

New product or service identification process

In my experience, new ideas can come from anywhere inside or outside the organization. Marketing can and should be sensitive to the market's needs and expectations as well as newly identified problems that can be solved in their markets. However, the *piece de resistance* is to provide meaningful products or services that no one ever thought possible through an understanding of what target customers value!

With technology products and services, there usually are ongoing R&D programs in areas of potential improvements or breakthroughs. However, I argue that the impact of these programs will be greatly enhanced by the technical team's level of exposure to the use of current products, the needs expressed by customers, the problems they experience (angst) and, most importantly, the customers' values. When the engineers and scientists, along with marketing - and often sales, service and other parts of the organization – have a clear understanding of these points, it enables more focus on the most important and effective developments that will make the greatest difference in the market.

As mentioned earlier, in times past, I've made a point of bringing our engineers out to spend time with customers as well as bringing customers into the company to speak with our technical staff and other members of the organization. This can be done one-on-one or by organizing internal symposia around what customers and marketing think are the topics where the greatest technology product or service impact can be made. Of course, the technical staff also should be attending professional meetings where customers present and/or companies exhibit, as another source of knowledge and ideas.

Some other sources of ideas are:

- **Current markets and customers** – Look for angst, understand customer values, understand competitions' weaknesses, answer the question *"what can our customers have that they never imagined was possible and will be compelling?"* An example is Apple's advance from the iPhone to the iPad.

- **Current markets and customer sub-market segments** – This could cover accessories, complementary products, consumables and disposables, among other possibilities. Another way of thinking about this is to provide a complete solution – remember the days of "batteries not included"? One obvious example is the printer and ink variation on the old razor and blade concept; *"give away"* the printer to sell the very profitable, continuously-consumed ink.

- **Adjacent product markets** – Look for opportunities in markets where your current core competencies port well into an adjacent market or segment. A low-tech example is when Nike decided in 1995 to branch out from shoes to golf apparel, balls, and equipment. Four years later, the move was scored as phenomenally successful, according to Harvard Business Review.

- **Adjacent geographic markets** – If you've created a success model at various levels, it could be replicated at whatever levels are appropriate in another geographic area. An A.D. Little paper cites Holland Bikes as a successful example of a company that annexed the French market. They did it by investing two years studying how French customers approach buying city bikes, adopting promotional programs to fit, training their people, and overcoming dealers' barriers to carrying Holland Bikes. Also, at the time of writing in 2015, Netflix is in the process of expanding their U.S. success model to other geographic markets.

- **Moving up the value chain** – Higher value products and services can be developed, acquired or facilitated by partnerships, but best when done without competing with current customers – for example, should a chip supplier to phones come out with their own phone? One example reported by VentureBeat.com is MisFit Wearables. They make sensor products for consumers that monitor sleep and activity. Their current focus provides ample customer feedback and opportunity for product improvement. Once the initial product has been established, their move up the value chain (while annexing an adjacent market) will come when they enhance these products for medical applications.

New product or service verification process

While market research can be important in the idea discovery process, I think it is more powerful in the verification process discussed below. There are a range of verification methods I've used that were effective in different situations.

- **Telephone interviews** – It is worth repeating here a technique discussed earlier that we've used successfully. First identify about 15 or 20 target customers, and then make a list of about five key questions that you believe are the most important ones to help you better understand your target customers' needs and expectations. Now call each one, introduce yourself and the fact that you're doing a survey related to a planned product or service offering – remember, you are not selling anything at this stage of the process; you are seeking knowledge and advice. Ask them if they can spare 15 minutes to respond to your five questions. Almost always, folks will say yes. It is worth noting that Rob Adams in his book *"If you build it, will they come?"* suggests that the number of target customers to survey is 100. If this is a market that is new to you or the product or service is very complex or the investment is extremely high, then consider that more might be better. In Rob Adams' book, he also suggests repeating the interview process as the concept evolves and becomes refined; it's an idea that could be valuable with either the same group of interviewees or different ones each time.

As you move through the questions, the respondent may introduce new ideas, comments or other information that is valuable, but not related to the specific questions. I've found that by just following this new thread, major insights and ideas were gained. After 15 minutes, if more time is needed, I always ask if they can continue another five or ten minutes; it shows deep respect and appreciation for their time. After speaking with about 10 or so respondents, a pattern begins to emerge; additional calls tend to support the emerging pattern. The information gained will help shape your thinking about their needs and expectations as well as introduce some new ideas. It may lead to more work to better understand this area, or it may be sufficient to move forward with the next steps in your plan.

- **Personal discussions** – If you know target customers or have a way to meet them, great insights can be gained from such meetings, especially if one is prepared with questions and a process similar to the telephone technique above.

- **Focus groups** – These are usually done by professionals who conduct them on a regular basis. Their value seems greatest when a product or service is pretty well defined but would benefit from more clarity at the user level.

- **Published market reports** – I've found these to be good sources of data about the markets, customers and competition. By themselves, their value is limited, but they help to fill in a lot of important, broader information needed to paint the full picture.

- **Market surveys** – They provide a data set from a specific audience about specific questions. The difficulty I've found is getting the questions right, especially when there is a new product or service idea that needs to be validated. One significant challenge; is in the respondents' ability to understand the new idea sufficient to enable them to provide a meaningful answer; or perhaps more accurately, the challenge is for the surveyor to enable the respondent to adequately understand the new idea.

- **Customers who provide advice and evaluation** – These are target or existing customers, "thought leaders" and Innovators who are using gold-standard competitive products and early adopters who understand enough about the technology or its application to be valuable sources of input, ideas, refinements and verification as the idea evolves from concept to bench top to prototype to alpha and beta units. They are *"Innovators"* and *"Early Adopters"* in Rogers' parlance from his book on *Diffusion of Innovations*, described in the next chapter below.

I can't say enough about how valuable this can be with technology products. In a large nuclear medicine instrumentation company where I worked, we followed this entire process through to the initial product beta-testing stage, where upon these customers would receive the product on consignment (with some favorable future buyout terms) in order to gain daily experience, publish papers and speak at symposia or society meetings. By the time the products were shipped to other customers they were well refined and we had customers selling customers – there is no better marketing program than your customers doing it for you!

New product or service rollout

The best model, in my opinion, is based on the work of Everett Rogers in his book *Diffusion of Innovations*. His book incorporates much earlier work from numerous researchers. It is best described in the chart and explanation below that is based on Rogers' book. The chart shows the diffusion process from left to right. Note that Rogers' chart is enhanced to show that with successive groups of customers adopting a new technology blue), its market share (yellow) will eventually reach saturation level.

The fundamental concept in both the below chart and its summarized description is based on the work of Everett Rogers' *Diffusion of Innovation 5th edition*, Free Press, 2003

To put the chart in perspective, Rogers points out that the chart and descriptions are "idealized", that there are no distinct breaks between target customer categories, and that it is essentially a continuum. That said, he further points out that there are <u>distinct characteristics</u> in each of the categories.

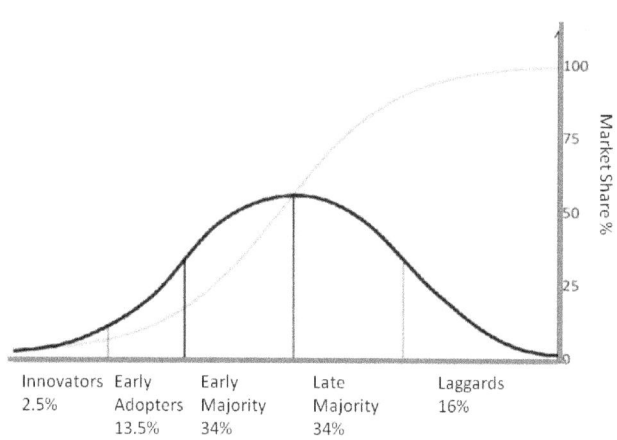

Source:<u>https://en.wikipedia.org/wiki/File:Diffusionofideas.PNG#filelinks</u>

<u>Innovators (2.5%)</u> – Innovator customers' role is to import into the market system the new ideas from outside the system's boundaries. The Innovator's profile is that they are:

- Obsessively venturesome; risk takers

- Developers of peer relationships with other Innovators in their field regardless of geography

- In possession of financial resources they control, which facilitates risk taking while limiting downside consequences

- Able to understand and apply complex technologies

- Opinion leaders and change agents, we have found, who have access to exogenous funding and a desire to share knowledge; however, because they are not considered main stream in their work, they remain somewhat at the fringes of their market system.

Note that the company's relationship with this group needs the participation of responsible managers. They would include product development, marketing, sales and possibly other functional areas; while the relationship must be led by a team leader who can work with the Innovators, earn or maintain their respect and manage the process. The team and its leader will need a budget and appropriate authority to provide the Innovators with early stage product, support and modifications as needed.

Early Adopters (13.5%) – This group earns the respect of peers through their successful, practical application of new ideas. They maintain their esteemed position by carefully selecting and demonstrating the real-world use of new ideas; they provide the "stamp of approval".

The Early Adopter's profile is that they are:

- Geographically local in their relationships and communication

- Viewed with the highest degree of opinion leadership, implying they have knowledge and experience

- The person to check with by the Early Majority or near peers when considering adopting a new idea

- Not too far ahead of the mainstream in innovativeness; thereby serving as a role model

This group represents an opportunity for marketing professionals to facilitate maximizing Early Adopter's impact on their near peers and the Early Majority – e.g. use as a "local missionary". We've used Early Adopters in symposia, sponsored publications and presentations of papers at professional meetings, as a few examples.

Early Majority (34%) – They take time to consider or deliberate decisions about adopting innovative products or services. The following quote used by Rogers on page 267 of his book sums up the Early Majority:

"Be not the first by which the new is tried, nor the last to lay the old aside." Alexander Pope, *An Essay on Criticism,* 1711.

The Early Majority's profile is that they are:

- Adopt new ideas just before the average mainstream target market

- Interconnected with peers, but are not considered opinion leaders

- An important link to the next target market groups: Late Majority and Laggards

From our experience, they are the group most influenced by the marketing professional's efforts to facilitate communicating the Early Adopters' experience.

Late Majority (34%) – Individuals in this category will adopt an innovation after the average member of the market system. These individuals approach an innovation with a high degree of skepticism.

The Late Majority's profile is that they are:

- Limited financial and other resources

- Risk averse; need to be "safe"

- Their susceptibility to fear, uncertainty and doubt (FUD) will be higher than previous groups

- In a category that may adopt out of economic necessity and/or peer pressure

Laggards (16%) – Laggards are the last to adopt an innovation; long after they have become aware.

The Laggard's profile is that they are:

- Traditionalists that associate with other traditionalists

- Looking to the past as their point of reference

- In possession of very limited financial and other resources

- Inclined to distrust new ideas and change

- In need of a high degree of certainty that adoption of a new idea will not fail

The above work is a generalized model where some experts believe that people or organizations that might fit a particular category under one set of circumstances may not fit in another set. Where our team has had good knowledge of markets, especially in health care, it has not been difficult to find the Innovators, Early Adopters and Early Majority, as well as the remaining two, for our purposes.

While we have had significant success with this model, the key has been in placing special emphasis on the Innovators. Apart from the obvious, offering some form of recognition and reward for their risk and their willingness to serve as opinion leaders has been important. For example, in the field of nuclear medicine, we worked with our market Innovators to refine our ideas and developments. The evolution to having them serve as beta test sites was natural, if not expected by them. While the instruments were often consigned at no initial cost, there usually was an attractive buy-out price after some extended evaluation period. These innovators would break established patterns to try something new, then publish papers on their experience and speak at symposia and other events where their knowledge and experience was well received by the next category: Early Adopters.

It is worth noting in the nuclear medicine example that the Innovators were most easily found in research and/or teaching hospitals, although some were in the most prestigious, large general hospitals. Some of these Innovators could get research funding or grants to be able to conduct application-related studies that used these new products being tested at the beta stage, which was a bonus to them. Usually, it was an individual Innovator or their immediate team who were the champions or passionate advocates for their involvement with us.

As our market for new products evolved, additional passionate advocates were sought from the early adopters and early majority. They would be respected leaders whose work was specialized in specific fields of diagnostic clinical medicine, such as cardiology, neurology and oncology. We had a professional education department that would organize symposia wherever needed as part of our market development program. It was highly successful and a valuable service to our prospective customers as well as the sales organization.

In another example, a company that I helped found, we located several beta test candidates in hospitals for trying a computerized learning process that would replace the required annual training that was traditionally done in classroom style. The hospitals were in a competitive environment, but the real champions were senior human resources managers responsible for training who saw this new process as a way to save significant money, improve both productivity and employee morale by not sitting in a classroom for a day, have proof of regulatory compliance and have a more effective learning and evaluation set of tools. They were change agents in this case. They were offered the computer based learning product and support for half price, plus full support and upgrades for two years. In exchange, they would allow the company to obtain comparative data that would quantify the economic and quality benefits of this product. In addition, they would welcome prospective Early Adopters to speak with them or even visit to see first-hand their results to provide validation of the value proposition. In this case, there is a great deal of competition along with the attendant drive to improve productivity within health care; so once a few leading or well-respected institutions started using this product, they all had to have it! From the standpoint of personal motivation, responsible decision makers had the opportunity to timely adopt this product and earn respect for the benefit brought to the hospital; or not, which might be hard to explain.

Market Introduction and Development Phases
Shown in Terms of the Rogers' Innovation Diffusion Model

Last Target: Laggards
They make a <u>Necessary</u> decision
•No risk
•Replacement
•Provide organized support
•Show all the proof of efficacy
You must <u>Guaranty that it works</u>

Beta Test: Innovators
They make a <u>Creative</u> decision
•"Like us" customers
•Subject matter leaders
•Provide personal support
•Provide incentives
•Collect data
You must <u>Make it work together</u>

Main Target: Early and Late Majority
They make a <u>Tactical</u> decision
•Low risk
•Improvement or replacement
•Provide organized support
•Show proof of efficacy
•Collect more proof of efficacy
You must <u>Prove that it works</u>

Market Entry: Early Adopters
They make a <u>Strategic</u> decision
•Risk takers
•Change agents
•Provide organized support
•Collect proof of efficacy
You must <u>Show that it works</u>

The chart above, whose diagrammatic proportions are approximations, maps my experience at the "30,000 foot level" into Everett Rogers' *Diffusion of Innovations* models' labels in order to make several key points.

One point is the way our markets seem to have evolved through the basic needs each of our customer groups exhibited. The Beta Test or Innovator customers were responsive because they had a need to create, whereas our Market Entry or Early Adopter customers made a strategic decision as change agents. Then our Main Market or Early and Late Majority customers made decisions that were more discretionary and tactical than strategic. Finally the Laggard customers made necessary tactical decisions – they had no choice but to buy something. Each group was approached differently, and there were some things we did that are also shown on the chart. For example, at each stage is the risk profile from Innovator to Laggard expressed as **Make it Work, Show that it works, Prove that it works and finally Guaranty that it works**. These labels parallel each groups':

- Acceptance of or avoidance of risk, and
- Need for or resistance to change.

A complementary resource covering the product or service roll-out strategy and process, is the book *Crossing the Chasm* by Geoffrey Moore (HarperCollins Publishing, 2002). This book is in my view a generalized model and resource for high-tech products and services that are intended to serve mainstream customers. In it he covers in detail both the profile and the methodology for reaching each stage of target customers through the entire adoption process. In addition, it covers product promotional strategy, product positioning and other relevant topics. One high-level takeaway is the book's use of the D-day analogy, where the entrepreneur is asked to think like General Eisenhower when he planned and executed the allied attack on Normandy in June of 1944.

Advertising, Promotion and Publicity

As an introduction, these activities create awareness and support planned or actual selling. They differ yet complement each other in that:

- Advertising is paid communication to your target market using mass media. It enables targeting specific messages with unlimited creativity and repeatedly. The cost per "impression" or "eyeball" is generally low. However, its effectiveness should be measured to ensure that the tool is cost effective; especially because there is no other feedback than either inquiries or actual sales. Advertising's overall cost is very high, however, because usually one is reaching a very large audience.

- Promotion refers to either programs for the selling channel, such as bonuses or prizes to sales personnel; whereas, promotion directed at the consumer usually comprises special offers or coupons.

- Publicity offers a way to get exposure at no or low cost. Media will publish a news release or do a story on a new technology or a product of high interest. The media providing the publicity may expect that you will be advertising through them.

Takeaways from this chapter on Marketing:

- Simple definitions: Marketing is creating demand; Sales is fulfilling demand

- New products or services identified by understanding customers' needs, expectations, problems and values; new products or services range from incremental improvement to breakthroughs never thought possible

- Target and existing customers are the most valuable resource for verification of a new idea using a range of tools at different times in the process

- The *Diffusion of Innovations* adoption model serves as a high-level guide for how to lead and manage the new product or service adoption process

- The Market Introduction and Development phases chart and text enhance the adoption model's process

Resource recommendations for more detail on this Marketing chapter:

- Adams, Rob. *If You Build it, Will They Come?* John Wiley & Sons, 2010.

- Blank, Steve. *Why the Lean Start-Up Changes Everything.* Harvard Business Review, May 2013.

  https://hbr.org/2013/05/why-the-lean-start-up-changes-everything/ar/1

- Moore, Geoffrey. *Crossing the Chasm*, Harper Collins Publishing, 2002

- Rogers, Everett. *Diffusion of Innovations.* New York, Free Press, 5th edition, 2003

Sales

Since this book is intended to be accessed for specific topics as well as read, the following text is a repeat from the Marketing chapter.

I've observed that the terms marketing and sales are often used interchangeably. My own simple definitions are:

- Marketing: Creating demand

- Sales: Fulfilling demand

While this may seem an oversimplification, and it is to a certain extent, it is a very convenient way to see what must be done, how it must be done and who must do it. One illustration is that in a past corporate experience, the sales organizations worldwide were totally separated from the products-producing "factories" that also had marketing responsibility. It was often difficult to be effective in these conceptually complementary if not symbiotic roles. The reasons were that each party would not be able to consistently respect the boundaries of the other that should have enabled them to be much more effective together.

To put a little more color on the subject by repeating from an earlier chapter, the site BusinessDictionary.com offers the following definition for <u>marketing</u>:

"The management process through which goods and services move from concept to the customer. It includes the coordination of four elements called the 4 P's of marketing:

- *Identification, selection and development of a **product**,*

- *Determination of its **price**,*

- *Selection of a distribution channel to reach the customer's **place**, and*

- *Development and implementation of a **promotional strategy**."*

To compare the term <u>sales,</u> the same source provides the following definition:

- *"The activity or business of selling products or services.*

- *An alternative term for sales revenue or sales volume."*

One take away is that marketing is both strategic and tactically enabling (supportive); while sales is more tactically than strategically the act of matching prospective customers with product or service offerings and closing the deal.

Still, even largely tactical effort must be guided by strategy or "doing the right thing, before trying to do the thing right". A simple illustration is the old saw about people hacking their way through dense jungle growth. One member climbs a tree and declares: "Stop! We're going the wrong way". Another on the ground shouts back: "No, we should keep going, because we're making great progress".

Sales Strategy

Selling scenarios can have many different forms. Here are four basic scenarios that simplify the development of an effective strategy. The three charts below, in their original form, were copyrighted by Sales Development Associates.

Transactional Selling - The simplest form is Transactional Selling, which is akin to what you find in retail stores and on the Web. I want to buy an item now that I need now and will pay for it now, if you have the size, brand, etc. that I need. Interestingly, even here I've observed sales clerks can often benefit from effective training to understand their products and manage a fairly straight-forward process. An example to consider is buying off-the-shelf items at Best Buy, such as printer ink or flash drives.

Problem Solving - This is where the product or service is complex, but the decision is simple – e.g. one decision maker. For example, an engineer is designing a circuit requiring specific functions, specifications, reliability, large quantities and a defined price point. The problem to be solved is either finding the right product solution to fit the need or designing one to meet the need. This type of selling requires an engineer who can understand the customer's total requirements and connect with his or her own company's engineers or product managers.

Consensus Building - In this scenario, the need is simple, but the sales effort requires dealing with a complex organization. A good example was with the computer-based learning company mentioned earlier. The product enabled training to take place at an individual's convenience using either a company computer or one's own computer. Thus, it replaced expensive and less efficient classroom training. While this was a very straightforward product for the HR folks who were the training leaders, in some cases it involved some of the managers of staff who were going to be trained, regulatory affairs, finance, IT and senior management. Therefore, the sales person had to be trained in the product, of course, but also had to manage the customer's team and the purchasing process. The type of selling and the training, skills and profile of this category of sales person is dramatically different from the two previous scenarios.

Organizational Consulting – It combines the challenges of Problem Solving and Consensus Building. An example from my experience was when we were seeking host hospitals to have our cyclotron and radiopharmacy in their facility where we'd manufacture short-lived radiopharmaceuticals for both their needs and regional distribution. Regional distribution was provided to facilities needing the drug for diagnostic imaging tests, but didn't need or want a cyclotron and radiopharmacy in their hospital. The problem solving part included: where to put it in the building, how to construct an arms-length relationship, licensing and regulatory compliance, among others. The consensus part typically included, of course, the physicians and department heads that would use or benefit from the products produced at our facility in their hospital, senior management, finance, regulatory affairs and legal.

As the reader might imagine, this took knowledge and skills that were at a high level in being able to solve the various problems while managing the process through the organization. It also required managing a strong support team, as no one person either could have all of the information or do it all.

Sales Strategy Matrix

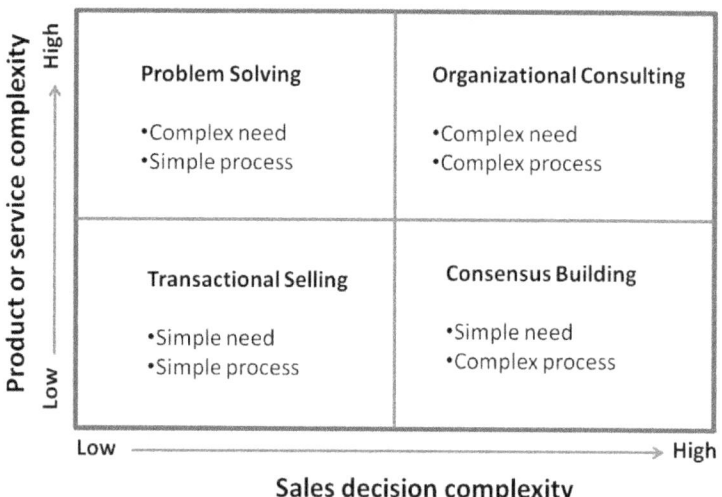

The Sales Strategy Matrix above contrasts the product or service's complexity with the sales decision's complexity to show the selling strategy for each in bold. The light text describes the tactical structure of the process.

Different scenarios require specific profiles in the selling effort to be optimally effective. Imagine someone who is an expert in the technology and its application trying to successfully sell to a large organization where the buying process is very complex – without additional training and skills in organizational and process management, the chances of success are just that: chances.

Sales Strategy Matrix – Buyer's Behavior

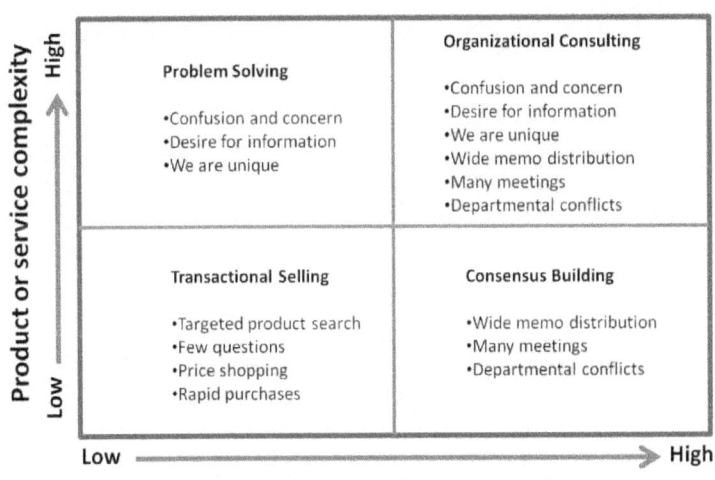

Sales Strategy – Buyer's Behavior

By repeating below the strategic selling categories from the chart above, the light text shows the prospective buyer's environment. The challenge for the sales person or team is to address each of these tactical issues.

Sales Strategy – Seller's Behavior

Once again by repeating the strategic selling labels, the tactical issues that the seller must employ are shown in the light type.

Sales Strategy Matrix – Seller's Behavior

Product or service complexity (High / Low)	Sales decision complexity (Low → High)	
Problem Solving •High discovery •Educate the customer •Tailor your solution •Team selling •Lead qualified support resources	**Organizational Consulting** •High discovery •Educate the customer •Tailor your solutions •Team selling •Lead qualified support resources •Manage communications and resources •Build many relationships	
Transactional Selling •Make buying quick and easy •Know the answers •Demonstrate value •Differentiate yourself •Stand alone collateral material	**Consensus Building** •Build many relationships •Show political sensitivity •Resolve conflicting needs •Manage communications and process •Know the answers	

Transactional Selling - Building on the previous points, in this case the Buyer's Behavior will comprise either a targeted search or an impulse purchase resulting from browsing. Either way, the process likely will be similar with few questions, concern about price and the purchasing transaction executed quickly. Looking at the next chart covering Seller's Behavior, some ideas on how to be more effective in "managing" the relationship with prospective buyers starts with making the buying process quick and easy. Ways to accomplish that include:

- Trained sales clerks or floor staff – an example is where stores like Best Buy have knowledgeable and trained sales personnel who can demonstrate products and address prospective customers' questions.

- Stand alone collateral material – here a specification sheet or brochure that anticipates the needed information and answers to questions prospective buyers have will quickly assist in overcoming the bane of any sale: fear, uncertainty and doubt.

- Differentiate yourself – staying with the store example, one way is by having a complete selection. For example, at Best Buy one can find not only a range of core products, but all of the needed accessories and complementary products as well.

- Rapid checkout – it is a constant mystery as to why customers are often found standing in long lines waiting to give the store their money after spending time finding the items they will purchase.

In summary, one basic guideline is simply: "make it easy and folks will buy".

Problem Solving – Here the key ingredients are understanding and then recognizing the customer's unique situation, information sharing and collaborating on finding the best solution. The process will often call for subject matter experts to support the lead sales person, who must manage that process as well as the customer interface process. Some points that would improve the success probability are:

- Qualified lead sales people – in a technology field, they would likely be knowledgeable and credentialed on the subject; but they'd also be trained in managing the selling process as well as support resources. One interesting qualification might be to use Stephen Covey's fifth habit in his 7 Habits book: "Seek first to understand; then to be understood". How many people do you know that presume to have the answer when they don't fully understand the question?

- Qualified sales support people – supporting subject matter experts who, in addition to their knowledge and credentials, would need some level of training to be able to work as a team member in the selling process. Often these folks are primarily working in engineering, R&D, service or manufacturing. As a result, "they don't get out much"; therefore, they need coaching and training to be effective in a situation where raising your own objections or introducing information that triggers customers' fear, uncertainty or doubt can kill the sale instantly. For example, telling about a new, better product that is in development instead of focusing on the products being offered. Another common issue is bringing up problems with the current product that presumably are being addressed, but raise doubts. In any case, you see the picture.

- Quality sales support or collateral material – these are specifications, brochures, top-notch presentation materials for sales and support team members, manuals, customer testimonials and pre-approved customer site visits.

Consensus Building – This is a scenario where the sales person must lead the process through the customer's "jungle". Much of our nuclear medicine instrumentation sales were in this category. However, a successful sale almost always depended on having an internal "passionate advocate" or champion to move the rest of the organization in the direction of a favorable decision. The passionate advocate candidate is generally one who will not only benefit from a purchase, but is in a leadership position. A couple of passionate advocate leadership examples are heads of functional parts of an organization or a "natural" leader who has deep, well respected technical or other knowledge. The sales effort will often follow the passionate advocate's lead, since he or she is the champion.

Things that will enable a high success ratio are:

- Sales lead people who understand organizational dynamics and can relate well to people in responsible positions. In addition, the ability to question, listen, understand, coach, support and when necessary take the lead are more important than product or technical knowledge.

- A strong support team that can be used for presentations and meetings with diverse customer team members who are all recommenders and influencers if not decision makers in the purchasing decision process. These supporting team members might be subject matter experts who, in addition to their knowledge and credentials, would need some level of training to be able to work as a team member in the selling process. Often these folks are working in engineering, R&D, service or manufacturing.

- Quality sales support or collateral material – these are specifications, brochures, top-notch presentation materials for sales and support team members, manuals, customer testimonials and pre-approved customer site visits.

Organizational Consulting – This scenario combines all of the characteristics of Problem Solving and Consensus Building above. It obviously represents the most challenging selling scenario, but offers the opportunity to serve as a competitive barrier and provide a high return on sales effort if done well. It is worth the effort for either high price products and services or low price ones where the business is automatically repeated – e.g. consumables or disposables.

In summary, these Sales Strategy Matrixes show that the requirements for successful technology and services selling, when supported by effective marketing, can reduce adoption and diffusion times for new and existing products and services. Referring to Geoffrey Moore's *Crossing the Chasm* concepts, sometimes getting from one level, such as the early adopter to the main market, can be as simple as having a very effective marketing and sales plan with very effective execution.

I recently discussed a local early-stage technology company with a former colleague. He lamented that this company had a large target market, two powerful compelling reasons to buy combined with a patented differentiating advantage that was significant. Yet they just couldn't get beyond the occasional sale. In the discussion, it was clear that to both of us that their barrier to growth was an effective marketing and sales plan that would need to be well executed. By developing a winning plan, then the other missing ingredient can be addressed – more capital. The likelihood of raising additional capital is certainly better when there is a viable plan and pathway to success.

By the way, right now, this company's current investors are squabbling about their investment and lack of returns; they are not focused on the issue of getting to success. Thus, it suggests a need to step back with the investors and board to re-evaluate or develop a shared vision. Doing so will likely win support for the new marketing and sales plan. However, without a shared vision, it's hard to imagine the investors and board supporting anything new.

This example is also instructive because the two compelling reasons to buy are so strong that the prospects are located at a much earlier time throughout either the *Diffusion of Innovations* or the *Crossing the Chasm* models. This observation supports the notion that these models are useful in a generalized form, but must be adapted to each situation.

Distribution Channels

It's beyond the scope of this book to address in detail market channels, because the needs of any specific technology based product or service will require a tailored approach. However, it's worth pointing out that the options are:

- **Direct selling through your own sales force.** This is likely the ideal approach for industrial or B to B products and services. It also is needed for customers who fit the description of Organizational Consulting, Problem Solving and Consensus Building. Direct selling requires hiring, training and supporting qualified employees. While it is the most expensive, it provides the highest level of control over the selling process.

- **Selling via intermediaries**. This approach is a lower cost alternative for industrial and B to B products and services. It typically uses "manufacturers' representatives" that are independents who represent a range of companies and products that serve a particular market. While the cost to enter is fairly low, since they are already working in your field, they will require training and support. My experience has been that they respond proportionately to attention and tender loving care. The downside is that they are going to sell the products or services in their portfolio that are the easiest and produce the greatest compensation.

- **Selling using structured intermediaries**. This approach is suited to retail consumer products. Intermediaries include retail stores and e-commerce channels where the selling process is transactional. In the case of stores, training and support materials are essential for enabling the sales personnel to identify, qualify, present and overcome objections to close a sale on the floor. By contrast, e-commerce is mono-directional; that is, there is little if any opportunity for dialogue. The product or service presentation must sell it for you. However, reportedly in the U.S. since 1999 there are now roughly 10x more people online, and online revenues from e-commerce and advertising have risen 15 times.

Takeaways from this Sales chapter:

- Simple definitions: Sales is fulfilling demand; Marketing is creating demand

- Different selling strategies are needed for transactional, problem solving, consensus building and organizational consulting sales scenarios

- Tactically, the seller's behavior must complement the buyer's behavior in each sales scenario

Recommended resources for more detail on this Sales chapter:

- Care, John and Aron Bohlig. *Mastering Technical Sales: The Sales Engineer's Handbook, 3rd Edition.* Artech House. 2014

- Johnson, Mark W., Greg W. Marshall. *Sales Force Management 11th Edition,* Routledge, 2013

- Kee, K.B. A Dozen Things I've Learned About Marketing, Distribution and Sales, *Bamboo Innovator,* May 29, 2014
  http://bambooinnovator.com/2014/05/29/a-dozen-things-ive-learned-about-marketing-distribution-and-sales/

- Onyemah, Vincent, et al. What Entrepreneurs Get Wrong. *Harvard Business Review*, May 2013
- https://hbr.org/2013/05/what-entrepreneurs-get-wrong

- Wax, Ken. *The Technology Salesperson's Handbook: 114 World Proven Lessons and Tactics*, January 27, 2011

Raising Capital

Raising capital is beyond the scope of this book to address comprehensively, but some thoughts and experiences are worth sharing because they may serve to clarify or advance any capital raising effort.

Simple Wealth Creation Model

Sell product or service Deliver value, get money	**"Do stuff, get money"** Create wealth, build company

Offer Product or Service Create value for target market

Raise Capital •Non-dilutive grants •Loans •Equity investors	**Market's Innovators** •Alpha or beta product •Work with Innovators •Make it work together

"Get money, do stuff" Idea Talent Capital

One of the most common and surprising is that many entrepreneurs who are at the stage of needing capital decide that they want to maintain maximum ownership, which by itself is not an unreasonable expectation. However, I have observed some waiting to get to the ultimate deal while the market's window of opportunity slips slowly away. Otto

Wheeley, the founder of the East Tennessee venture capital firm Venture First, roughly said *"It's better to have a moderate piece of a large pie than a large piece of a tiny pie"*. He also said *"When you see a turtle on a fence, you know that he didn't get their by himself"*. Obviously, the point these quotes illustrate is that we need to share the risk and share the benefit when seeking investors or partners in our entrepreneurial businesses. And, we all need some help in addition to capital, which quality investors can bring in many forms, since they usually bring a lot of experience and contacts while are sharing both the risks and the benefits over time.

Stages of Development – Capital Sources Scenarios

In the technology fields there is a generalized pattern of how capital is raised. It starts with the notion of "get money, do stuff" and transitions for successful folks to "do stuff, get money"!

- **Early stage development** – low risk development (see chapter on Stages of Technology and Manufacturing Risks). Money can come from anywhere: you, friends, family, angel investors, SBA loan, grants or even crowd sourcing. Other than a loan or a grant, one ingredient for inspiring potential investors is to take the time to discuss your vision, with the expectation that they will internalize it and share it. The next step is to discuss your plan for success.

Since the reader knows friends and family well, here are some thoughts. Angel investors are often successful people who either have knowledge and experience in your field or they are interested to "give back" something to innovating entrepreneurs to help them also achieve success. In addition, there are early stage angel investor groups that can be accessed. When we have done this, there was one person from such a group who did preliminary due diligence and served as an entrée into the group for a meeting or presentation. In general, they are risk takers, but the risks should be in proportion to the benefits to be attractive. One should expect some significant level of due diligence to be performed, and any claims will need to have reasonable proof to support them.

- I have had some recent limited experience with crowd funding. A friend's organization was raising money for their worthy cause, and based on my recommending potential sources for their field crowd funding has been effective for them.

- **Mid-stage development** – above very low risk development. Small Business Innovative Research (SBIR) grants, other government grants from NIH, NCI, Army, Navy, etc. Unfortunately, much early stage, high risk development work is done under grant funding; whereas angel investors, venture capital investors and strategic corporate investors and partners are more interested in investing where there is less risk and a pathway to success. Our experience with SBIRs was very good. In one company, we had a 50% success rate in winning SBIRs and other grants, partly because we knew the various program managers and what they wanted. Fortunately, our needs and theirs often aligned. I've worked with some early stage companies who are really SBIR and grant companies who never get to a product or service that can be commercialized – i.e. they never get beyond the "get money, do stuff" stage - not a good business model.

As shown in the above chart, Simple Wealth Creation Model, some of the Innovators described in the Marketing chapter should be actively collaborating in your effort to prototype the product or service. This will aid in both improving the product's value proposition and in raising capital – they can provide "verification" of the market's potential and the ultimate product's probability of adoption.

- **Alpha and beta customer product** – angel investors and venture capitalists are candidates. Angel investors may be willing to take more risk with the expectation of higher reward downstream, as discussed above.

Venture capital investors, in our experience, are looking for a pathway to commercialization and the likelihood of a large return. Consider the earlier discussion about the level of risk in completing the development, manufacturing the product and then commercializing it successfully in the market. Appeal is going to be relative to the risk/benefit ratio – obviously, higher is better.

Also, we learned what we believe to be the venture capital model. We felt that VCs looked at every 10 investments with the expectation that two would be super stars, five would do OK, and three would fail. However, the long term, overall return from such a portfolio would be ~30% per annum. Of course, *a priori*, it's impossible to know which ones will be which; thus the portfolio concept is similar to any other risk-management and investing approach. Nevertheless, one key to our securing venture funding was mainly to have a pathway to success for a compelling product. It had strong differentiating advantages protected by a moat and a large target market. In addition, the key pieces were identified or in place and the risks were mostly known, even though some surprises were still possible. Another key was to have the plan, supporting facts and their proof readily available for the extensive due diligence process that accompanies serious consideration of an investment.

Venture capital organizations tend to specialize in fields where they have knowledge and experience related to either previous investments or partners' experience. In addition, geographic location is often important. We learned that it is not unusual for a venture capital organization to strictly limit the distance they are willing to travel to meet with one of their portfolio companies. One day round trip, including meeting time is not atypical. Others, however, are more interested in the technology or field of use, so travel time is less important. The takeaway is to do homework to find the best candidates.

How to make contact effectively can be murky. We have had success by getting exposure at meetings or expos where companies are invited to present their business plans to prospective investors. There are quasi-government organizations, among others, whose charter includes job creation and growing the state/county/city's economy. There are also individuals who are charged with finding and facilitating similar job creation and growth opportunities. In our state of Tennessee, we have organizations like Tech2020, Launch TN and our Commissioner of Economic Development, appointed by our pro-business-development governor, who serve in these capacities. These resources, as well as other contacts in the investment or business community can be sources of recommendation to a candidate venture capital organization that fits your profile. Such contacts can play a valuable role, since VCs are bombarded with business plans constantly; yet somehow the need to sort out the top prospects – and that is where a contact they trust can be valuable.

It's also worth mentioning that having a "talking dog" can capture prospective investors' imaginations faster than all of the business plans and slides one might be able to present. A talking dog, or demonstration product if you prefer, can be a bench-top demo or an alpha unit or even a similar product currently available used to show the current level of performance followed by something that shows what yours will do. Still, if you had an actual customer using an alpha unit or working with you as an Innovator to develop you product that would add more depth to your investment appeal.

- **Revenue and growth** – in this case, the risks may be more market and scalability related. Of course, venture capital is more readily available at this stage than any of the pre-revenue stages, but if it isn't a subsequent round from earlier investors, the terms may be tough. An alternative is a strategic partner willing to invest for reasons that go beyond pure returns. For example, a major player may be interested in licensing the technology in the future for specific fields of use. Another reason could be to consider the company as an acquisition candidate in the future. We've found that corporate strategic partners only seem interested at revenue stage or above; below this stage there is more risk with questionable benefit.

- **Revenue, profit and growth** – At this stage the options for raising capital are obvious. Initial public offering, debt, strategic partnership among others.

The brief article by Benedict Evans, cited at the end of this chapter, points out that while funding is up fairly steadily since 2009 the number of IPOs since 2000 has fallen. The cause for the IPO drop is mainly because later stage funding of high-growth tech companies has moved from the public to private markets. Funding sources for these companies now include hedge funds, private equity and conventional public market investors.

For entertainment, the following story from an unknown source is offered on the question of "Then what?"

A venture capitalist (VC) was at the pier of a tiny coastal village when a small boat with just one fisherman docked. Inside the boat were several large tuna. The VC complimented the fisherman on the quality of his fish and asked how long it took to catch them. The fisherman said, only a little while.

The VC asked: Why didn't he stay out longer and catch more fish? The fisherman said he had enough to support his family's immediate needs. The VC asked, but what do you do with the rest of your time? The fisherman said, "I sleep late, fish a little, play with my children, spend time with my wife, stroll into the village each evening, sip wine and play guitar with my friends. I have a full and busy life."

The VC scoffed, "I have a Harvard MBA and could help you". You should spend more time fishing and with the profits buy a bigger boat. Then with the profits from the bigger boat, you could buy several boats, so eventually you'd have a fleet of fishing boats. Instead of selling your catch to a middleman you'd sell directly to the processor, eventually opening your own cannery. You'd control the product, processing and distribution. You'd need to leave this tiny coastal fishing village and move to a larger city; and then eventually to NYC where you will run your growing business."

The fisherman asked, "How long will this all take?" To which the VC replied, "15-20 years." The fisherman asked, "Then what?"

The VC laughed and said that's the best part! When the time is right you would announce an IPO and sell your company stock to the public and become very rich - you would make millions!

The fisherman intrigued said: "Millions? Then what?" The VC said, "Then you would retire. Move to a tiny coastal fishing village where you would sleep late, fish a little, play with your kids, spend time with your wife, stroll to the village in the evenings to sip wine and play your guitar with your friends."

The moral of the story might be *"do you know yourself?"* The most interesting entrepreneurs to me are the ones who create products or services for reasons grounded in their deep conviction that something must be done in a better, faster, cheaper way; yet balanced with the need to create a viable and profitable business. Of course, their effort is framed in taking the steps that will most likely be successful and as a consequence create wealth. By contrast, those whose pursuit is driven mainly by the desire to either create wealth or "just make money" seem to have a much rougher road to navigate. In other words, the answer to the question about knowing yourself might lie in the answer to a different question: *"Are you doing it for the right reasons?"*

Takeaways from the Raising Capital chapter:

- Early stage development – most likely sources are friends and family, grants, crowd sourcing

- Mid stage development – most likely sources are grants, crowd sourcing, venture capital, possible strategic partnerships

- Early revenue – most likely sources are venture capital, strategic partnerships

- Predictable revenue and growth – mezzanine financing, venture capital, IPO

Recommended resources for more detail on this Raising Capital chapter:

- Jordan, Jeff et al. 16 Startup Metrics. *Andreeson Horowitz*, downloaded August 24, 2015. http://a16z.com/2015/08/21/16-metrics/

- Wilson, Fred. Burn Rate. *AVC*, downloaded August 24, 2015. http://avc.com/2011/12/burn-rate/

Raising Capital

Business Plan

There are numerous good books and articles on the subject of effective business plans. In times past, we read many and tried to optimize our plans to particular needs. One distinction for us was the difference between a strategic plan and an operating plan (strategy versus tactics or "do the right thing; then do the thing right").

The strategic plan was valuable for our companies in providing a high-level assessment of our business, plus it provided a high-level roadmap. The plan was valuable also for external presentations, whether presenting at investor meetings, providing prospective investors with a plan or recruiting talent. Still, when implementing a plan, surprises appear that require timely adaptability and modification of the plan.

Some ideas are offered about the strategic plan.However, the reader can add any level of tactical details to create an operating plan. Three things we've found to be critical in thinking about creating a strategic plan's claims, facts, projections and other information:

- Clear and crisp – easy for non-specialists to understand. If you really know your plan, it can be passionately communicated in a clear, concise manner

- Can be verified – the basis for statements are available and serve as "proof"
- Can be validated - the "proof" can be substantiated

To illustrate, in one of our business plans we made market projections by various segments. Some of the data came from published market research while the rest came from our own market research – by making all of these sources available upon request, they served as proof of our claims about our target markets. Then, by making customers and non-affiliated market experts available upon request, they provided validation of the proof. Essentially, a solid plan based on solid facts and sources will not only reflect the reality, but will support the credibility and trustworthiness of the businesses senior management team.

In business, lawsuits are to be expected unfortunately; however, one important lesson learned from the attorneys with whom I have worked is that the case is won before it ever goes to court through preparation - the courtroom is the "staged" performance. I believe the same maxim is more or less appropriate when raising capital – be prepared. With proper preparation, the business plan and related presentations become both easy to prepare and convincing when read.

Business Plan – Key Elements

The purpose of the Executive Summary is to "get to the meeting" with prospective investors. The purpose of the business plan detail is to both serve as your business roadmap and obtain any needed investment by providing sufficient depth with a pathway to verification and validation of the plan's key claims.

Topics we covered in our plans were the following:

- **Executive summary** – The first paragraph has the "grabber" – what problems are we solving and why is it exciting! Then it briefly covered vision, mission, strategies, objectives, market size, competing alternatives and business potential plus the pathway to becoming cash flow positive – all of these points supporting the "grabber". The Executive Summary should end with what you want from and investor

- **Target market overview** – Its background and the problem that we would solve

- **Product or service we'll offer** – A brief summary of current and future products or improvements

- **Target customer profile** – Including an assessment of what our customers value

- **Compelling reason to buy** – Why will they our product or service

- **Differentiating advantages** - For your product or service

- **Performance, price and form factor requirements** – Why and any deficiencies and solutions to resolve

- **Barriers to our market entry** - Solutions to overcome barriers such as regulations, competing products' patents, "moats", market channel(s) selection, etc.

- **Barriers to protect our market from competition** - e.g. patent protection, "moats", trade secrets, first mover advantage, sales force investment, regulatory, tax advantage, and/or other barriers

- **Risks** – What they are and how they'll be mitigated or retired; e.g. technology, manufacturing, market and financial

- **Trends** – Ones that affect current relevant business environment (externalities); e.g. consumer, regulatory, demographic, etc.

- **Competing products and services** - thorough, relevant analysis of all current and emerging competition. Covered leaders, market share, strengths and weaknesses

- **Competing technologies** – Indirect competition

- **Internal and external champions** – Technology, manufacturing, marketing or sales champions in your company; also, customers or Innovators who passionately support your product or service

- **Requisite core competencies** – What are they, why important and note any deficiencies and how they'll be corrected

- **Marketing and selling plan** – Channels, strategies, and tactics including pricing and promotional;

market assessment and sales forecasts based on solid data, information and/or credible assumptions

- **Pro forma financial plan** – Profit and loss, cash flow and balance sheet based on realistic market assumptions from above. Include needed capital and expected burn rate. An upside, median and downside plan can be valuable.

- **Liquidity options** – Address whether management sees investors being able to exit their investment by the company being acquired, going public, staying private with dividends or having some other liquidity outcome; "exit" plan is avoided because it has a negative connotation

Business Plan Presentation Questions

Anyone reviewing our plans or participating in a presentation always had questions. A few that the reader may encounter and be worth preparation are the following:

1. On any topic, how do you know that you know?

2. What are the obstacles and solutions to retiring technical, manufacturing and market risk?

3. How will you know if the business strategy is not working?

4. What would you do if the strategy doesn't work?

5. What are the key risks or uncertainties and how they will be mitigated?

6. Who would be your next staffing hires?

7. How will you attract and retain needed talent?

8. What is your current "burn rate"?

9. What is your time to market?

10. What is your current capital structure?

11. Is senior management committed? Are they sharing risk in order to share the benefit?

Every business plan is tailored to the needs of the business and the intended audience. Hopefully, the above ideas will contain some "gems" to include in a plan that may make a difference in the success of the business. Even if any of these ideas never get formally included in the plan, the thought process associated with them, used internally, may also be valuable.

Takeaways from the Business Plan chapter:

- Preparation will make the plan and related presentations easy and convincing

- Plan should be clear, crisp, verifiable and validatable – i.e. understandable and credible

- The purpose of the Executive Summary is to get to investor presentations – it should start with the "grabber" and end with what you want from an investment

- The purpose of the Business Plan is to both serve as your roadmap and obtain any needed investment by providing sufficient supporting detail that is both verifiable and validatable

- Business plans are just that "plans" – when surprises come, timely adaptability is needed

Recommended resources for more detail on this Business Plan chapter:

- Entrepreneur Magazine's Business Plan Books:http://bookstore.entrepreneur.com/product-category/business-plans-planning/

- Entrepreneur Magazine's Business Plan Pro Software Tools: http://entrepreneur.businessplanpro.com/?utm_sour ce=entrepreneurcom&utm_medium=BusinessPlans &utm_campaign=inlinebody

- Hendricks, Mark. Do You Really Need a Business Plan? *Entrepreneur,* December 2008 http://www.entrepreneur.com/article/198618

- Jordan, Jeff et al. 16 Startup Metrics. *Andreeson Horowitz,* downloaded August 24, 2015. http://a16z.com/2015/08/21/16-metrics/

- Vannelli, Steven and Eric Bush. "The Knowledge Effect: Excess Returns Of Highly Innovative Companies", *Seeking Alpha,* May 11, 2015

- http://seekingalpha.com/article/3167886-the-knowledge-effect-excess-returns-of-highly-innovative-companies

- Wilson, Fred. Burn Rate. *AVC,* downloaded August 24, 2015. http://avc.com/2011/12/burn-rate/

Business Plan

Getting to the Vision - Do the Thing Right

Have you noticed that when things don't get done either correctly or on time there are a menu of excuses, which may be valid, that are offered. Often the reasons are that something was missing that was needed to timely complete the task correctly. Dr. Edwards Deming famously cited management as the cause of a large percentage of the problems in business; and as he aged that percentage seemed to increase to 95%. My experience concurs with his observation, but it also appears that a significant percentage of the "management problems" are communication problems.

In the broadest sense, communication problems can be information or material or anything else that is needed for timely task completion. In a startup company, time is never your friend. Whether the issue is running out of capital before becoming cash flow positive or some competing technology advancing faster than yours or first mover advantage evaporating, it's hard to argue against team members having everything that they need to do their jobs.

Related to that point, Robert K. Greenleaf's book *Servant Leadership* describes the concept of leaders and managers becoming servants of team members needs. In the

145

foregoing material of this book, most of the work focuses on Doing the Right Thing. However, when it comes to implementation, effectiveness and efficiency come into play.

Consider a simple case where a team member is charged with getting something from A to B, whether it is a development task or a report or anything else; its execution requires a process and the principle is the same. After the obvious leadership or management questions of the qualifications of the team member are satisfied, then the questions become what does the team member need and when does he/she need it and who will supply it? If these questions and their answers are not just clear but supported by functioning systems or processes to meet those needs, what will happen? Will the task be timely completed to meet the need?

The role of a leader or manager in Greenleaf's concept is to ensure that all team members have what is needed to succeed and to know that the underlying support or input processes are working. Thus, the leader or manager becomes a servant of the processes that support every team member's responsibilities. The Process Model chart below, based loosely on the work of Phil Crosby, is as much a mental model as it is a useful working document. If one at least is conversant with the concept that it illustrates, it will be easy to detect dysfunctional elements of a process in order to correct them.

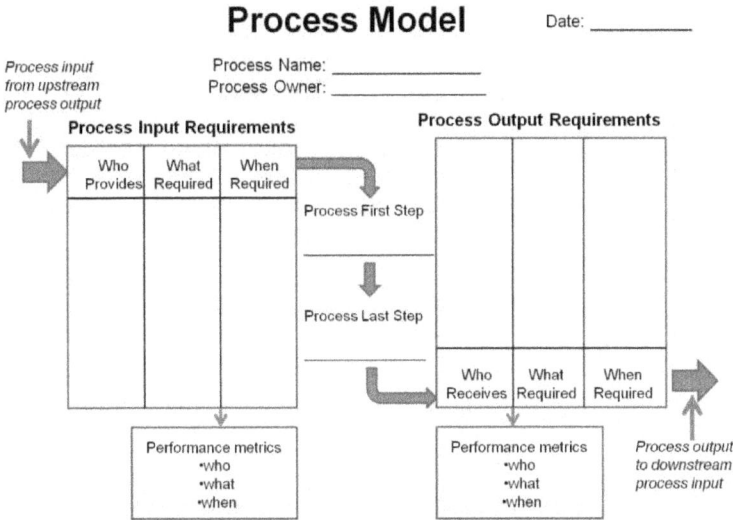

Sometimes, it is useful to write things out when working with team members, thereby elevating awareness of how their process works and sensitizing them to be clear on not only their needs to succeed but how the downstream processes depend on their output. Perhaps one example to illustrate how important this can be is in the case of first tier automotive suppliers. These companies are under contract to supply the right part at the right time meeting the right specifications – failure is not an option, because the penalties for each day they cannot perform are at least onerous if not crippling to their business.

In the above model, the following brief explanations may be helpful:

- Process name and owner: This is the process segment that supports a larger process. It has one owner who is responsible, accountable and presumably has the authority to execute within this framework.

- Process input: Even the first segment of a larger process will have in input such as requirements or specifications. Most processes are dependent on the one or more preceding or upstream processes' output(s) to provide them with what this process needs.

- Process first and last steps: This is a way of defining the point of demarcation between the preceding and the succeeding processes.

- Process Input Requirements: This covers simply who will provide everything needed on what schedule to enable this process owner to timely succeed in getting to the required output.

- Process Output Requirements: This may be the most important set of who, what, when requirements because they help define the input requirements. In other words, starting with the "end in mind", as Steven Covey suggests, and working back to the beginning of a larger process will enable each individual process to support the end goal.

- Performance metrics: The concept is to measure what matters for both the inputs and the outputs. If one knows what is working and what is not working, corrective action can be taken by the "leader as servant" to enable the team member to "do the thing right".

Of course, in start-up technology companies, things are often messy and change sometimes occurs frequently. Still, the Process Model presented above can be useful, even if it is just used as a mental guide to ensure that the right questions are asked and addressed as one winds their way through the development and commercialization stages. In more established companies, for the intrapreneurs, this model can be equally valuable for all of the above reasons, of course, but also because processes deteriorate due to many causes. For example, something is changed elsewhere in the organization that has an unanticipated effect on the larger process or a process segment. By applying the Process Model principles and monitoring the measurements that matter, deterioration will be detected early and before much damage is done.

Another advantage of the Process Model implementation is that for more established companies, it breaks down the barriers between functional groups and individuals; such barriers or "silos" are remarkably disabling. For both the entrepreneur and the intrapreneur minimizing if not eliminating individual and departmental silos can help keep the organization working as an integrated team.

Team Selection and Motivation

Since we're on the subject of people it might be useful to the reader to share the three Cs when hiring people or partnering with complementary organizations.

- **Competence** – Perhaps this is the most obvious criterion. Certainly employees must have the requisite knowledge and skills for their area of responsibility. Often I think of knowledge and skills as grounded in "science" while job execution is an art. One without the other likely won't make a productive employee.

- **Character** – Can this person be trusted to carry out given responsibilities with their associated authority? Will this person be loyal to the vision and mission of the enterprise? Are they committed to solve tough problems or will they "jump ship" as soon as a seemingly better opportunity presents itself?

- **Culture** – Will they fit in with the operating style of our company? For example, are we comprised of largely individual contributors or are we more team centric? What kind of personalities work best together in our company? Do we value creative people who challenge the current thinking or do we want people who don't question what we are doing and follow orders?

Once hired, the HBR article titled Employee Motivation below suggests that there are four key motivators that must be <u>collectively</u> satisfied to maximize employee retention and performance.

- **Drive to acquire** – Essentially having the options that rewards from performance provide

- **Drive to bond** – Basically the need to affiliate and identify with pride in part or all of an organization or team

- **Drive to comprehend** – This is about more than understanding, but more about meaningful achievement or "self actualization" in Maslow's terms

- **Drive to defend** - It's the need to feel secure and confident in one's beliefs and commitments; unfulfilled it leads to fear and resentment

The Employee Motivation article recommended below provides clear and comprehensive insight into each of these points, supported by credible examples.

This subject could comprise an entire chapter if not an entire book, but the purpose here is to provide a simple mental model that can be recalled and applied to the specifics of your situation each time a new hire is being considered. The team and its leadership are the center of gravity for success.

Takeaways from the Getting to the Vision chapter:

- Every task to be accomplished will require a process

- Defining the task and its input and output requirements enable employees to do their job efficiently and effectively

- Leaders and managers become servants by ensuring employees have everything needed for their process to be timely executed

- Employees can be evaluated, hired and/or positioned based on the "3Cs": Competence, Character and Culture

Recommended Resources for more detail on this Getting to the Vision chapter:

- Covey, Stephen R. *The 7 Habits of Highly Effective People: Powerful Lessons in Personal Change.* Simon and Schuster. 1989

- Covey, Stephen R. *Principle Centered Leadership,* Summit Books, 1991

- Greenleaf, Robert K. *Servant Leadership,* Paulist Press, 2002

- Nohria, Nitin, et al. Employee Motivation, *Harvard Business Review*, July 2008.

- Scholtes, Peter R., Brian L. Joiner and Barbara J. Streibel. *The Team Handbook, 3rd Edition,* Oriel, Inc., February 2003

References and Resources

Adams, Rob. *If You Build it, Will They Come?* John Wiley & Sons, 2010.

Blank, Steve. Why the Lean Start-Up Changes Everything. *Harvard Business Review*, May 2013. https://hbr.org/2013/05/why-the-lean-start-up-changes-everything/ar/1

Branson, Richard. Richard Branson on Crafting Your Mission Statement. *Entrepreneur.* Web. July 22, 2013. http://www.entrepreneur.com/article/227507

Care, John and Aron Bohlig. *Mastering Technical Sales – The Sales Engineer's Handbook, 3rd Edition.* Artech House, 2014

Carroll, Rory. Silicon Valley, *The Guardian*, June 28, 2014. http://www.theguardian.com/technology/2014/jun/28/silicon-valley-startup-failure-culture-success-myth

Covey, Stephen R. *The 7 Habits of Highly Effective People: Powerful Lessons in Personal Change*. Simon and Schuster. 1989

Covey, Stephen R. *Principle Centered Leadership,* Summit Books, 1991

Deneffe, D et al. *Overcoming the Real barriers to Entry into Adjacent Markets*, A.D. Little, January 2010

Dunkley, Mike. *"Why we need to move up the value pyramid for health tech",* VentureBeat.com. October 16, 2014. http://venturebeat.com/2014/10/16/why-we-need-to-move-up-the-value-pyramid-for-health-tech

Evans, Benedict. Thirty Five Years of U.S. Tech Funding. *Benedict Evans blog.* August 12, 2015. http://ben-evans.com/benedictevans/2015/8/12/35-years-of-us-tech-funding

Gallo, Carmine. *The Four Elements of an Inspiring Vision.* Bloomberg Business. November 25 2008. http://www.bloomberg.com/bw/stories/2008-11-25/the-four-elements-of-an-inspiring-visionbusinessweek-business-news-stock-market-and-financial-advice

Grayeff, Yigal, Apple Inc. *(AAPL), Seeking Alpha,* http://seekingalpha.com/news/2623855-apples-dominance-of-profit-almost-complete

Greenleaf, Robert K. *Servant Leadership,* Paulist Press, 2002

Hendricks, Mark. Do You Really Need a Business Plan? *Entrepreneur,* December 2008
http://www.entrepreneur.com/article/198618

Hermann, Ned. *The Creative Brain.* Brain Books, September 1, 1989

Hull, Patrick. "Be Visionary; Think Big", *Forbes,* December 19, 2012
http://www.forbes.com/sites/patrickhull/2012/12/19/be-visionary-think-big/

"IBM PC DOS", *Wikipedia,* July 2, 2015
https://en.wikipedia.org/wiki/IBM_PC_DOS

IPhone. (2015, July 16). *Wikipedia, The Free Encyclopedia.* Retrieved 17:20, July 16, 2015.
https://en.wikipedia.org/w/index.php?title=IPhone&oldid=671637079

Johnson, Mark W., Greg W. Marshall. *Sales Force Management 11th Edition,* Routledge, 2013

Jordan, Jeff et al. 16 Startup Metrics. *Andreeson Horowitz*, downloaded August 24, 2015.
http://a16z.com/2015/08/21/16-metrics/

Maslow, Abraham. "A Theory of Human Motivation." *Psychological Review* (1943).

Moore, Geoffrey. *Crossing the Chasm*, Harper Collins Publishing, 2002

Nohria, Nitin, et al. Employee Motivation, *Harvard Business Review*, July 2008.

Onyemah, Vincent, et al. What Entrepreneurs Get Wrong. *Harvard Business Review*, May 2013
https://hbr.org/2013/05/what-entrepreneurs-get-wrong

Rogers, Everett. *Diffusion of Innovations*. New York, Free Press, 5th edition, 2003

Scholtes, Peter R., Brian L. Joiner and Barbara J. Streibel. *The Team Handbook, 3rd Edition*, Oriel, Inc., February 2003

Smartphone. (2015, July 14). In *Wikipedia, The Free Encyclopedia*. Retrieved 17:19, July 16, 2015, from https://en.wikipedia.org/w/index.php?title=Smartphone&oldid=671457902

Smialek, Jeanna. Here's How Much Technology Is Messing Up Our Most Important Measurements of the Economy, *Bloomberg Business*, July 28, 2015. http://www.bloomberg.com/news/articles/2015-07-28/here-s-how-much-technology-is-messing-up-our-most-important-measurements-of-the-economy

Stahl, M.J and Gregory M. Bounds, *Competing Globally Through Customer Value*, Quorum Books, 1991

Vannelli, Steven and Eric Bush. "The Knowledge Effect: Excess Returns Of Highly Innovative Companies", *Seeking Alpha*, May 11, 2015 http://seekingalpha.com/article/3167886-the-knowledge-effect-excess-returns-of-highly-innovative-companies

Vision Statement resource: http://www.lifehack.org/articles/work/20-sample-vision-statement-for-the-new-startup.html

Wax, Ken. *The Technology Salesperson's Handbook: 114 World Proven Lessons and Tactics*, January 27, 2011

Wilson, Fred. Burn Rate. *AVC*, downloaded August 24, 2015. http://avc.com/2011/12/burn-rate/

Woodruff, Robert B. and Sarah Gardial. *Know your customer- New Approaches to Understanding Customer Value and Satisfaction*. Blackwell Publishers. 1996.

Zook, Chris, and James Allen. "Growth Outside the Core." *Harvard Business Review* 1 Dec. 2003.

About the Author

During Don's career he has lived and worked every chapter in this book. He cofounded a Sarnoff Technology Venture Company for infrared detectors, a consulting company for early-stage technology businesses, and a manufacturing and distribution company for short-lived radiopharmaceuticals used in diagnostic tests. He also served as an officer in an early stage company that led the development and adoption of positron emission tomography (PET) for diagnostic imaging. He assisted the founders of a computer-based learning company that was acquired and a digital imaging company that went public. He was a member of a mentoring board for technology startups and co-founded an information technology accelerator.

He served in large, mid-size, early-stage and start-up technology companies, including American and German in the U.S. and French and Belgian in-country. Don's had responsibilities in technical design, writing, testing, quality, international sales, operations and worldwide marketing. He has also held senior management and leadership positions in sales, marketing, quality, regulatory affairs, business development, and European operations; and as co-founder, board member, CEO and chairman.